HAUNTED EL RENO

TANYA McCOY AND WHITNEY WILSON

Published by Haunted America
A Division of The History Press
Charleston, SC
www.historypress.com

Copyright © 2019 by Tanya McCoy and Whitney Wilson
All rights reserved

Cover image taken by Tanya McCoy.

First published 2019

Manufactured in the United States

ISBN 9781467141550

Library of Congress Control Number: 2019943355

Notice: The information in this book is true and complete to the best of our knowledge. It is offered without guarantee on the part of the authors or The History Press. The authors and The History Press disclaim all liability in connection with the use of this book.

All rights reserved. No part of this book may be reproduced or transmitted in any form whatsoever without prior written permission from the publisher except in the case of brief quotations embodied in critical articles and reviews.

This book is dedicated to the city of El Reno and its inhabitants, current and former, for opening up about the history of your city and for all of the new and exciting things to come.

To my oldest daughter, Tessa McCoy, and my mom, Gwen McCoy.
—*Tanya McCoy*

To Tanya McCoy for being my bestie, pushing me to do things I normally wouldn't do and tolerating my generally unpleasant disposition.
—*Whitney Wilson*

CONTENTS

Acknowledgements ... 7
Introduction ... 9

The Jensen Home ... 13
El Reno Carnegie Library ... 19
Elks Lodge #743 ... 22
The Centre Theater ... 25
Irving Elementary School ... 30
Rose Witcher Elementary School ... 32
Haunted Houses of El Reno ... 34
    Whitney's Houses
    Tanya's Ghostly Encounter
    Other Hauntings in El Reno Homes
The Canadian County Museum ... 48
Haunted Highways of El Reno ... 57
    Dead Man's Curve
    The Hunchback of Route 66
    Ghostly Route 66
    Foreman Road—Between Yukon and El Reno
Fort Reno ... 62
    The Welcome Center at Fort Reno
    The Cavalry Museum at Fort Reno
    The Chapel of Fort Reno

Contents

The Victorian House at Fort Reno
Fort Reno Cemetery
Lake El Reno   84
The Southern Hotel   87
The Whistle Stop Saloon   92
Downtown El Reno and Main Street Hauntings   94
Haunted Rock Island Avenue
The Bakery
The Main Street Office
Bickford Avenue
The Heritage Apartments   102
The Old Canadian County Jail   104
El Reno Cemetery   107

Bibliography   109
About the Authors   111

Acknowledgements

We would like to give a special thanks to the Canadian County Historical Museum; Pat Reuter; Vicki Proctor; Judy Mihn; El Reno Main Street; Debbie Harrison; the mayor of El Reno and Carnegie Library; Tommy and Amy Neatherly of El Reno; the Oklahoma Historical Society; the Elks Lodge of El Reno; Cortney Kane Sides; Jennifer Handley; the City of El Reno; Heather Brothers; the National Cavalry Museum; Wendy Ogden; the Fort Reno Historical Society; Jim Johnston; Ron Cross, founder of Paranormal Research of Organized Studies; Chris Smith and Mike Goncalves of the Tennessee Wraith Chasers; Kale Epperson and Jeri Beavers of Paranormal Investigations of Oklahoma; Jeromy Jones, creator of Paranologies; Martha Hazzard Decker; Linda Anthony Hill; Gayle Early; our OPA Oklahoma Paranormal Association teammates Cara Pershall, Kelly Henderson and Dawn Green; Rylie Powell, former resident of El Reno; several contributors who wish to be left unnamed; and, of course, our wonderful and supportive husbands, Joshua Wilson and Clinton Womack-McCoy.

INTRODUCTION

For years now, it has been believed that Guthrie, Oklahoma, is the most haunted town in the state. Many people agree with that statement, but when we started researching *Haunted Canadian County*, we found a town that matches Guthrie, if not surpasses it, in ghostly activity. One only has to review the town's history to understand why it is believed to be so haunted.

Located due west of Oklahoma City, just off historic Route 66, sits the historic town of El Reno, which took part of its name from the nearby fort, Fort Reno. El Reno was first established shortly after the land run of 1889 and began to grow when the first railroad reached it in 1890. The Chicago, Kansas and Nebraska Railroad line (CRIP) extended from Kansas to Texas and soon became the largest employer in El Reno. In the same year, the town's first post office was established with a tent as its first, official residence. In 1890, the town had a population of 285. By 1900, the town had grown to twelve times its original size with a population of 3,383 residents, and by 1910, the population had doubled to 7,872. Around 1930, El Reno had twenty-four grocery stores, ten hotels, thirty-eight filling stations, twenty-four restaurants, twenty-four beauty and barber shops, thirty-six insurance companies and a multitude of other businesses. In the 2010 census, the population of El Reno was recorded at 16,749; the slowing down in growth is partially due to the bankruptcy of the railroad in 1980.

Another large employer in El Reno is the federal prison. Located two miles west of El Reno is a large federal prison, which was first named the Southwestern Federal Reformatory. It housed male inmates that were thirty-

INTRODUCTION

five years of age and younger. In 1934, the prison became the fifth largest in the United States. In the mid-1970s, the prison was renamed the Federal Correctional Institute of El Reno. It now houses male inmates of all ages and has become the clearing house for prisoners being transported across the nation. In 1990, the prison became El Reno's largest employer.

Today, El Reno has a diverse group of businesses, including Redlands Community College located on the far west side of town. Downtown El Reno still houses a multitude of historic buildings dating back the turn of the century; many of them are sitting empty just waiting for new businesses to arrive and once again breathe life into their red bricks. Historic downtown El Reno has a true life of its own. As you walk along its historic streets, you can almost feel time slip away to its long-forgotten wonder years of trolley cars and horse-drawn buggies that used to travel through El Reno. It's a truly a beautiful historic town, just a few miles away from downtown Oklahoma City, that is holding fast to some of Oklahoma's most precious history along with a few ghosts who are just waiting to share their stories with you.

Old Downtown El Reno. *Tommy Neathery.*

INTRODUCTION

John Allen's Auto Livery, Bickford Street. *Tommy Neithery*.

El Reno's first fire department. *Carnegie Library*.

Introduction

Davis Electric, downtown El Reno. *Carnegie Library.*

M.N. Wilson Furniture Store, 1908. *Carnegie Library.*

The Jensen Home

Thomas Jensen emigrated from Germany to America and settled in El Reno during the time of the first land run. In town, Jensen became a real estate developer and insurance dealer, and he played a prominent role in securing El Reno as the county seat during the legal battle between Frisco and El Reno. Jensen would soon be considered one of the town's founding fathers. In 1890, the territorial governor, George Washington Steel, appointed Jensen to the Board of County Commissioners to help organize Canadian County. He would later deed over eighty acres of his land to the city in order to help with its development.

Jensen's wife, Minnie, played an important role in helping to develop the education programs and other community-driven organizations. She often hosted the meetings at her own home, which was built by Thomas Jensen himself. The couple would spend the rest of their lives in that home, raising their family in the community that they had helped to build.

Nestled in a historic neighborhood in El Reno, their two-story home is supported by three tall, white columns that adorn the front of the house. Built in 1909 by Thomas Jensen, this gem of a home stands strong against the test of time while retaining its beauty and charm.

When you first enter the house, you are greeted by a spacious entryway that opens directly into the dining room area, which leads directly to a large kitchen. In the kitchen is a back staircase, which was used by the family's staff to reach the second floor of the home. To the right is a formal living room area with a small fireplace. One can only imagine the meetings and

Wade Street facing the old Jenson Home. *Tommy Neathery.*

teas that must have once been hosted in this small, formal sitting area. Just north of the living room sits another room. Now being used as a personal office space, it once held the personal wake of Mr. Jensen himself. In this room, located upstairs, Mr. Jensen passed away suddenly in his sleep of a heart attack.

To the left side of the home, you'll notice a beautiful staircase. The banister, made of hand-carved wood with an intricate design, guides your way up to the second floor with two small landings along the way. On the first landing, you will notice a small sitting area to your left. This small sitting area is where someone would sit to chaperone two sweethearts in case someone decided they might try to steal a kiss. Also located on that level is an ornate stained-glass window that adorns the external wall. As you ascend farther up the stairs, you will reach the second landing. Here, you will see a wall filled with historical pictures and articles collected by the home's current owners, Tommy and Amy Neathery.

As you ascend the last set of stairs, you will find yourself greeted by a small open area and a hallway that leads off to several rooms on the second floor. Directly to the right, you'll locate a small room with an exterior door that leads out onto the balcony. The room next to it is a little larger and houses a small library filled with various books that line the walls. As you travel down the hall, you will find the master bedroom, another guest room,

Jensen Home, present day. *Tanya McCoy.*

an upstairs bathroom and a smaller bedroom that is located at the very end of the hall. Across from the small bedroom, you will find the top of the staircase that descends into the kitchen below. Much like the wall along the upper staircase, the hallway wall is adorned with historical pictures detailing El Reno's past.

Tommy and Amy Neathery now own the home located off of East Wade Street. Tommy said that, even as a young child, he was always drawn to the old Jensen home. He would often pass by and stare at the house knowing, one day, it would be his. When he and Amy first started dating, their dates would often include driving by the old home and talking about what it would be like if they were ever able to purchase the place. Then one day, they did. Since then, they have made it their lives' work to try to restore and maintain the historical home's original beauty, even purchasing items that once adorned the original house. Despite the Jensen place's beautiful appearance, there are some ghostly tales that exist behind its wooden doors.

Prior to the Neatherys owning the home, the house was owned by another couple who had used it as a bed and breakfast, and one of the ghostly tales took place during that time. Located on the second floor, down the hall and in the very back of the house, sits a small room, which is believed to have belonged to the Jensen's housekeeper since it is located at the top of the servants' stairs. Every night, after all the guests had left, the previous owner would go through all the empty rooms to clean and make the beds. One night, when she returned to the old servant's room, the bed she had just made had an imprint on it as if someone had come up and sat on the bed. When she asked her husband why he had messed up her freshly made bed, he denied ever being up there. It was just the two of them in the home at the time.

Another ghostly tale took place when a different family was living in the home. The parents hired a baby-sitter one night to watch the kids while they were out of the house, and one of the girl's friends came over to keep her company. During the night, the friend went upstairs to use the restroom, and when she returned, she was so upset and scared that she ran out of the house vowing to never return. She never told the family what she had experienced that day or what she had seen. However, one witness has described what she saw in the house. Upstairs, in the doorway of the room that faces the stairway, the witness said she saw a full-body apparition of a man standing in what is now considered the library. When asked to describe what the gentleman looked like, the description the witness gave was very similar to that of Mr. Jensen. When showed a picture of Mr. Jensen, she confirmed that the man she saw standing in the doorway did in fact look like the man in the picture.

With all of the paranormal reports centered on this house, we asked Tommy and Amy if we could bring our team in to investigate their home. We wanted to see what activity we might be able to witness ourselves. They graciously agreed. We arrived early on a Friday evening. Storms were forming to the west of us as a bitterly cold north wind carried gray clouds our way. As we pulled up in front of the house, the clouds opened up and began to pummel us with large, cold droplets of rain. We grabbed our equipment and quickly ascended the steep stairs into the old home. Lightning lit up the sky, and the thunder seemed to shake the home from its wooden floors to its rafters. With all of the energy in the air, we were hoping for an active and productive night.

We set up the equipment and positioned ourselves around the downstairs area. It didn't take long for the activity to start. The first responses we received were from the living room area. A K2 meter (an EMF device used to pick up on electromagnetic or energy fields) that was set on top of the antique fireplace mantel was the first piece of equipment that picked up any activity. The original reading in that particular area was a simple baseline of one green light being lit up on the K2, but after Dawn, a member of our team, started asking questions for our EVP (electronic voice phenomena) session, we started getting responses. Upon request, the entity began to manipulate the lights on the K2 meter in response to her questions. This session lasted for several minutes.

Other pieces of equipment were placed around the home. A digital recorder was set on the dining room table, a night vision camera and a parascope were placed on the staircase and a 360-degree parascope was placed in the office area next to the dining room. We also had several devices running with a ghost radio and a ghost detector placed around the downstairs area.

Kelly, another investigator with our team, was sitting on the staircase when she heard what sounded like an old music box playing upstairs, just above where she was sitting. Around that same time, the 360-degree parascope started to light up. The parascope was sitting on the floor in the room that was being used as an office, the same room that once held the wake of Mr. Jensen while he lay in his coffin. The parascope remained lit with one red light for about five minutes. We started to address the entity that we believed was in the room at the time. We asked several questions, including, "Can you light it to yellow, then can you light it to green?" On demand, the parascope lit up. When we asked who we were talking to, we received a positive light response to the name Minnie, the name of Jensen's wife. We continued to have parascope activity for approximately twenty minutes, often with several colors lit up in one area for a long amount of time. It was more activity than I've ever witnessed before on any investigation.

After a short break, we resumed the investigation by sending Kelly and Dawn upstairs with our guests while Whitney and I stayed downstairs. Whitney and I settled in the living room area to give ourselves views into the office area, the dining room area, the entry to the kitchen and the entryway and the staircase. As our ghost radio continued to provide us with various words, we sat quietly in the dark and watched all the areas in front of us. I started taking pictures toward the office area, and I took a series of twelve, all in the same direction. Upon review, I noticed what appeared to be orbs present in two of the pictures. I believe that about 99 percent of what we believe to be orbs in pictures are not truly orbs but dust, bugs and possibly even spiderwebs. However, when you do capture an orb, they have distinct characteristics. They self-illuminate, they change directions, and they can also be seen with the naked eye. These orbs were captured by the room where we had previously had parascope activity and near the fireplace where we had the K2 activity, and they were captured not long after Whitney said she saw a shadow figure ascending the staircase.

I started taking more pictures, and this time, I took another series of twelve pictures toward the dining room area and the kitchen doorway. Upon reviewing the pictures, I noticed what appeared to be a light mist hovering above the dining room table directly in front of the kitchen doorway. When I zoomed in on the area, we were able to make out two faces. One appeared to be a man wearing a hat of some type on his head. Standing to his right, there appeared to be a shorter person who appeared to be a woman in a dress with her hair curled up and placed tightly to her head. They reminded me of a picture I saw on one of the walls upstairs. I ascended the stairs to look at the photo I had seen previously, and I noticed that the people in the picture closely resembled the couple in my photograph. I was sure that I had just captured a photograph of the Jensens, who were still keeping an eye over their once beloved home.

As the investigation came to a close, our team members that had investigated upstairs with the Neatherys joined us downstairs to talk about that night's investigation. Whitney and I were excited to share our findings, experiences and photos that we had caught downstairs with the Neatherys. I showed them the pictures I had taken, and they shared the experiences that they had upstairs. We were all in agreement that the Jensen home appeared to exhibit some type of paranormal activity. Amy and Tommy said they feel quite at home with the resident spirits; they never feel threatened or uneasy with the spirits in the home. The house itself has such a welcoming feeling to it; it feels as if you are visiting an old friend. It appears that, even after death, the Jensens continue to make their mark on history through their home in El Reno.

EL RENO CARNEGIE LIBRARY

Just off the main street in El Reno, there sits a building named the Carnegie Library. In 1902, the residents of El Reno petitioned the city council for a public library. Without the funds to build a permanent structure at the time, the council rented a space at the YMCA and paid the organization $25 a month to form the first library of El Reno. In 1903, after receiving a pledge of $12,000 from Andrew Carnegie, a rich iron tycoon, construction began on the present library building. Built in the Classical Revival style, the Carnegie Library is two stories tall and features four tall columns that stand in the entryway. The library opened its doors on March 5, 1905. Its original design housed the library on the first floor and a theater-style wooden stage on the second where local theater performances and high school graduations were held until 1912. The second floor was later converted to a children's library in 1927; in 1962, a basement was added for storage and in 1964, a fireproof archive was built to help store and protect thousands of historical pictures, newspapers and documents. Today, it is the oldest library in Oklahoma that is still functioning as a library.

As you ascend the stairs to the library and pass between the majestic columns, you are surrounded by shelves that are lined with books. History surrounds you as the smell of books and papers fill the air. As you walk in, you are greeted by an old wooden desk where many librarians have shared the post over the years. Above you, lining the walls and archways, are small, intricate flowers and vines that wind their way around the room. A large, white, granite staircase leads up to the second floor and waits for you to take the first step.

Carnegie Library. *Tommy Neathery.*

When entering the building, the first spirit I picked up was that of a lady standing in the stacks directly to my right. She was wearing a turn-of-the-century dress with a high, lacy collar. Her hair was dark and pulled up into a bun on the back of her head. She stood very straight and regal, her hands clasped directly in front of her, and she simply stared at me. I didn't feel threatened in any way, but I was sure the lady I was seeing had been a librarian at one time. She appeared to still be on duty, keeping an eye over her precious books.

As we walked farther into the building, I told the staff that I had picked up on a name: Mary. The staff wasn't sure who I was referring to at that time, but later that night, they would remember that one of the classrooms in the library was named after a patron named Mary.

Over the years, there have several reports of people feeling like they were being watched and never quite alone in the library, and some said they heard disembodied footsteps upstairs while they knew no one was up there. The night of our investigation proved to be no different.

We started our initial investigation on the first floor of the library. We placed various pieces of equipment throughout the area and turned on our ghost radio. After about thirty minutes of asking questions and obtaining very little in the way of responses, we decided to investigate the second floor of the library, the children's area. When we arrived, we heard what appeared to be the sounds of walking echoing through the building.

The second floor consists of a large, open area that contains several small bookshelves and tables with chairs. There was a different feeling on the second level than there had been on the first. Even though several of us were in attendance, there seemed to be someone or something else there with us. The first presence I felt was that of a young boy, no more than seven or eight years old. He seemed to be playful and was wearing a hat that resembled a herringbone, wool flat cap. His clothes appeared to be turn-of-the-century as well. It was if he was trying to play a game of hide and go seek with us. However, he was not the only spirit who seemed to be with us that evening. We soon noticed the presence of another entity.

Behind the wall of the old stage, there is a storage room that would have once been the back of the stage or dressing area. Now, it stores various things on its many shelves. When you walk through the room, you come to another door that steps down into another small room. This small room is now the back wall of the elevator shaft that was placed in the library not too long ago. Due to the electrical panel, high EMF levels are registered in this area. I felt a headache coming on and decided to leave that immediate area. When I was back in the storage room, I started to feel the presence of a female in the room. She seemed sad and very forlorn. I walked out onto the landing by the stairs and got an immediate feeling of uneasiness. A great sadness came over me that made me feel slightly dizzy. I reported my feelings to some of the some of the library staff members that were with us during the investigation. Several of them said that they had experienced the same feeling and would not venture into that area alone.

It was a short night of investigating, and we may never know who is currently haunting this historic library. However, we do know that there seemed to be several spirits there, still enjoying the library. So, if you need to find a good book to read, or if you just want to enjoy the spirit of the library, stop in and visit the oldest working library in Oklahoma.

ELKS LODGE #743

The Benevolent and Protective Order of Elks was started as a social club in New York City in 1868 by Charles Vivian. The Elks Lodge, as it came to be known, hosted social gatherings and performances for its members, and membership grew quickly, leading to requests for lodges in other cities. Vivian's vision for the Elks Lodge was a charitable one. Among some of the Elks Lodges' contributions are field hospitals they set up during World War I, loans and scholarships that they have provided for veterans returning from war, more than half a million pints of blood that they donated during the Korean War and letters they volunteered to write to soldiers during Operation Desert Storm. Of course, this isn't an exhaustive list; the tradition of charitable giving is carried on in individual lodges. From helping members in distress to funding scholarships for high school students, the Elks have a mission to make their communities better places.

The Elks Lodge in El Reno is a beautiful, three-story building with a basement. It was built in 1904 at the St. Louis World's Fair as a headquarters for the Oklahoma Territory to promote statehood. In 1905, the building was split up, brought to El Reno on the Rock Island Railroad and reassembled in its current location on Rock Island Avenue. The façade of the building was remodeled in the 1970s and remains the same to this day.

As you enter the lodge on the main level, you are greeted by a large, open ballroom area. Wooden floors line the hall, and tall white columns extend from the floor to the ceiling. Toward the back of the hall is a kitchen stocked with various dishes and glasses that are ready to be used for the

Elks Lodge, early 1908. *Tommy Neathery.*

next big event. Many people have reported hearing the dishes clanking and glasses being moved when no one was present. To the front of the hall is a small stage area where I sat for a moment to observe the ballroom. As I sat on the stairs and looked out onto the dance floor, I saw soldiers dressed in their uniforms take the arms of young ladies and lead them onto the dance floor. I could almost hear the band playing an upbeat tune as I looked out onto a sea of young couples enjoying the night. It was like I was watching a movie play out in front of my very eyes. Later, when I told our host what I had seen while sitting in the ballroom, she informed me that I was not the only person to have witnessed that, as others have also seen or felt the same thing in that area.

Farther into the building, there is a large, wide staircase that leads up to the next floor, and a beautiful stained-glass window can be seen adorning the wall. As you ascend the staircase, you come to a landing area where sets of stairs line both walls that lead you farther up onto the next level. The staircase to the right leads to an open room with a small bar area. In this room, wood paneling and mirrors line one of the walls, and if you look closely, you might just see the entrance to another small, wooden room. This secret room holds various items, from an old pool table to broken crystal chandeliers. What other secrets those walls might hold are unknown to us. On one of the walls in the room there is a picture of one of the Elks' past members. No matter how many times workers straighten the picture, it always tends to move.

People have reported feeling uncomfortable around the photo, like the man in the picture is staring at them. When we first walked up to the third level with our dear friend and host for the night, Cortney Kane Sides, we were all standing around and talking when I caught a movement out of the corner of my eye. I turned to look at the staircase that led up to that room and saw a middle-aged man walk up the stairs and then turn and walk into the room we had just come out of. I asked Cortney if anyone else was in the building, and she answered no. I told her what I saw, and we walked over to the room and looked in, but there was no one there.

We returned to the other side of the building as we continued with our tour. On the opposite side of the building is another set of rooms: one large room with a padlock on its door and a few smaller ones opposite that. The smaller rooms were mainly used for storage, but the larger room was more interesting. It was the meeting room for the order of the Elks and was closed to the public, which left an air of mystery surrounding it.

In the lower level of the building there are three primary areas: the open foyer, the game room and the bar. The open foyer sits between the game room and the bar, and in it there is a large round table with several chairs around it for people to sit and visit or perhaps play a round of cards. Next to the foyer, the game room plays host to several pool tables, a jukebox and various other games. In this room, there is another kitchen area that serves as the bar. Cortney confided in us that she doesn't feel very comfortable in that area and tries to avoid it whenever possible. There is a set of restrooms that are adjacent to the game room. Many people report a feeling of uneasiness in the women's bathroom, and some even refuse to look in the mirror out of fear of seeing someone or something else standing there. Many have reported feeling so dizzy when they first walk into the area that it almost causes them to feel disoriented.

On the opposite side of the building is a small bar. The room itself has several small tables with chairs set up around the room and a large bar area toward the back. Someone once reported that they were in the room by themselves when they heard noises coming from behind the bar. Shot glasses flying off the shelves have also been reported, and doors and chairs have been known to move on their own, as if being pushed by unseen hands.

Other stories have been reported as well; from missing objects to growls being heard, the Elks Lodge appears to play host to several types of hauntings. Despite whatever restless spirits haunt the Elks Lodge, the building remains a beautiful facility to host any event. Just make sure you place an extra table setting for any unseen guest who might wish to join the party.

The Centre Theater

The Centre Theater in El Reno, Oklahoma, first opened its doors on December 1, 1944. Built on one of the main streets in the downtown area, the Centre offered its patrons an exciting experience in the world of drama and comedy directly from movies that featured actors from Hollywood's A list. The theater spent several years empty until the city took over the building. Renovations were done, and once again, the Centre Theater was open for public use. For a short time, the El Reno Community Theater group held various stage productions in the building until it moved into the El Reno High School auditorium to do its productions. The city now rents out the location for events and hosts a classic movie night open to the public. From Humphrey Bogart's, "Here's looking at you, kid," to Katharine Hepburn's, "Oh, that's silly. No woman would ever run for president. She'd have to admit she's over thirty-five," the theater has brought a little bit of joy and romance into each patron's life

The Centre was constructed in an early art deco style and featured a small lobby and a concession area that were ready to greet everyone who showed up to enjoy an ice-cold Coke and popcorn. Guests would have been greeted by ushers as they entered the main auditorium of the theater. With almost seven hundred seats to choose from, they had their choice of seating. At the front of the theater is a medium-size wooden stage with a large movie screen stretching down from the ceiling. Blue-covered cushioned seats stretch from the floor up several sets of stairs to the old projection booth. It's in the projection area that our story begins.

Haunted El Reno

Old Rocket Theater, now known as the Centre Theater. *Tommy Neathery.*

When we first arrived at the theater, it appeared very small in size, but when I entered the building to gather some more information about its history, I was reminded of just how big the theater really was. Cara, one of my team members, and I met Heather Brothers, an employee of the City of El Reno, to take some pictures of the theater. As we passed through the glass doors that lead into the theater, it was like we were taking a step back in time. The art deco style was carried throughout the interior of the building as well as the exterior. The old concession stand is still in place as if it's ready to serve moviegoers. We were shown into the theater area, and even with all the lights on, the theater still appeared dim, which only helped to cast an eerie feeling around the room. As I made my way down to the front of the theater, I ascended the stairs to stand on the stage. When you stand on the stage, you can really get a sense of how large the theater truly is. Today, the Centre only seats 250 to 300 people, less than half the number it originally seated. I can only imagine how massive the crowds must have been during the Centre's glory days.

My first visit to the theater was several years before when I was looking for some local sites to host one of our paranormal events. I had heard that the theater was haunted, and I was curious to learn more about it. I spoke

The Centre Theater. *Tommy Neathery.*

to one of the members of the local theater group that was currently running stage productions out of the theater, and I asked him if he had heard or experienced any paranormal activity. He told me about a time he had been alone upstairs in the office area and heard a noise coming from the lobby area. He went downstairs to see who had come into the building, but no one was there. People often report seeing a man up in the projector room. On the day of my first visit, I took pictures around the sitting area. When I reviewed them, I was surprised to see what appeared to be a man sitting up in one of the blue theater seats looking down at us. There was not a man with us that day other than the theater representative, but he was standing directly next to us. Prior to taking the picture, we had heard some noises coming from up in that area, but we didn't think much about it until we noticed the man in the picture. Some people believe it may be the spirit of Red Slocum, a man who spent many years of his life at the theater and who reopened the theater in 1945 after a fire damaged the location.

Since our first visit, the team has been back to the theater to conduct a full investigation. On March 16, 2019, our group met up in El Reno to investigate, and we, along with guest investigators Kale Epperson, Jeri Beavers and a few guests from our meetup group, spent five hours in the historic building trying to see what evidence we could find. Before the lights had even been turned off, our group started getting activity through the equipment we had started setting up. We started our setup in the main auditorium area, which is a large, open area consisting of over two hundred blue seats lined up on a steep incline toward the projector room. At the front of the theater sits a large stage with a semicircle section projecting outward toward the seating area.

The team split up into three groups; one went to the upstairs manager's office, one went below the stage and the others went to the old projection room. I was with the group in the manager's office upstairs, and right away, we started getting interactions with our equipment. Whoever was up there didn't want us there, and they were not afraid to tell us. The establishment next door was hosting a special St. Patrick's Day celebration and had a Celtic ladies band playing music. The spirit decided it was too loud for him and started complaining "about the noise outside." He also informed us that we were in his way. Jeri had been standing near the door way when she felt someone push her as if trying to get past. We investigated the location for approximately thirty minutes before we moved on to the next area.

Our second location was in the basement area beneath the stage. It was a small room encased in cement. The room was empty except for one small desk located against the far wall. Dust lined the walls and floor, and a large amount of dead cricket carcasses were scattered across the floor. We had already witnessed a few shadow figures hanging around the stage area earlier that night, and while we were in the basement, we witnessed another one standing at the top of the stairs. We continued to get intelligent responses to our questions in the basement when I started feeling as if someone was playing with the hair at the base of my neck. I had been sitting on the cement stairs but decided to join the rest of the group in the room and tell them what I had been feeling. Kim, another guest with us that evening, made the statement that she too had felt someone playing with her hair but thought perhaps it was a spider. We looked for any sign of a spider or cobweb, but none were to be found.

Our next location was the old projection booth. Prior to the start of our investigation, many people were drawn to the area saying they felt some energy coming from the room. We set up our equipment, and once again, we started getting interaction. This time, whatever entity was interacting with us also started to use pieces of our equipment. The first pieces of equipment that started responding were our censor touch lights. No one was near them when they started to light up on their own. Next was our K2 unit, which we use to detect electromagnetic activity. The lights started to respond, and soon we were able to get the spirit to answer our questions through the lights. This went on for several more minutes until it was finally time for us to move on to our final destination.

Our last location to investigate that evening was in the main auditorium of the theater. For this investigation, the entire group was present. It would be in this location that we would experience more activity than we had all night. Right away, our parascopes started lighting up on and around the stage. One parascope stayed lit for about five minutes, moving the light between red and yellow, before finally turning off. The touch censor also kept responding while it was set up on the stage. We spoke to several entities that evening, one of which we ended up calling the Reverend since that's what he called himself. The Reverend even seemed to be giving us a sermon of sorts that pertained to Easter, which was coming up. This part of the investigation continued to go on for an hour, during which the spirits continued to interact with us until we packed up and left the building.

My group was not the only one that experienced activity that night. One of our groups, led by two of my team leads, Kelly Henderson and Dawn Green, reported that they had some interesting activity upstairs in the manager's office. They said they were interacting with a spirit who kept bringing up the color red, or at least they thought it was the color it was talking about. Little did they know that it was most likely one of the old owners, the one who reopened the theater after the fire, Red Slocum.

Overall, the Centre Theater did not disappoint us when it came to an investigation of this haunted location, and we can't wait to go back. So, if you are looking to catch one of your favorite movies from the years past in an amazing location filled with history, check out El Reno's Centre Theater. Just make sure to keep your eyes open for a chance to glimpse one of the spirits that still resides there. You never know who or what you'll see.

IRVING ELEMENTARY SCHOOL

On Foreman Road to the east of El Reno, there sits an abandoned school known as the Irving School. Prior to the Irving School being built on this site, another school, built between 1895 and 1898, stood in the same place. The current building, built in 1930, consists of an old gymnasium, a large auditorium with a stage in the center of it, eight classrooms, a principal's office and a janitor room that all total to be 13,610 square feet in size. The building was used as grade school until 1970 or 1971 when it was turned into a district-wide kindergarten that was considered the jewel of El Reno until it closed its doors. Due to the failing condition of the building and the cost of upkeep, the city decided to sell the building in 2000. When the building was purchased, it was turned into a private residence, and the classrooms were turned into studio apartments.

Several of the former residents say they experienced paranormal activity while living in the apartments. Jackie, a former resident of the apartments, shared her experiencing with me. She lived there from 2011 to 2017, and during that time, she had several experiences. She told me that she had a picture of Jesus that flew off the wall one day along with several other knick-knacks. Her husband said he also experienced his own paranormal activity. He was home alone one day when he heard noises in the apartment; when Jackie came home a little while later, he realized what he had been hearing couldn't have been her. Both Jackie and her husband said they often heard voices coming from the basement area when no one was there.

Old Irving School. *Tanya McCoy.*

Other past residents have also claimed to have heard disembodied voices and the laughter of small children playing out in the common area. Residents have said they often experienced an uneasy feeling as if someone was watching them.

The Irving School still stands today but is currently condemned. Trespassing is strongly discouraged and punishable by law. Please remember that even though this building appears to be abandoned, it may not be, and places like this can be very dangerous.

ROSE WITCHER ELEMENTARY SCHOOL

Built in 1949 or 1950, a blond brick building known as the Rose Witcher Elementary School sits just off Williams Avenue. The school was named after Rose Witcher, who was a long-standing resident of El Reno and a respected and loved teacher before her passing on November 1, 1973.

Rose Ollie Witcher was born on October 17, 1885. She was a schoolteacher for forty-seven years and a resident of El Reno for forty-two years. The school was dedicated to her on May 2, 1950, and it was the first school to have a green chalkboard. During the dedication, the superintendent, Paul R. Taylor, was quoted as saying:

> *During her years of service, Miss Witcher has influenced the lives of thousands of boys and girls towards high ideas and better living during her thirty-six years as a citizen of El Reno. Certainly, no person could be more deserving of the high honor conferred on her by the community in naming a school structure in her honor.*

Over the years, there have been two fires in the school. The first one occurred in 1973, and after an investigation, it was ruled an act of arson. The second fire took place in 1983 and was also ruled to be an act of arson.

Today, Rose Witcher School has an average of just over four hundred students and serves as a first and second grade elementary school with a twenty-to-one student-teacher ratio. It is considered an above-average school with great reviews from the parents.

Despite it being a pleasant school, it still has its own reports of paranormal activity. It is said that toilets there often flush on their own, doors close themselves and the lights seem to be turned off by unseen hands. Even though several people claim to have experienced paranormal activity in the school, they all claim to not be afraid or threatened by it in any way. In fact, many feel it's the spirit of Rose hanging around doing what she loved best, caring for the children of El Reno.

Haunted Houses of El Reno

Like those of most towns, El Reno's hauntings don't only exist in historic buildings; they exist in the private, residential homes as well. Some are historic and some are more modern, but both are equally capable of being haunted. Many people don't think about a newer home being haunted, but it's not only a home that can be haunted; the land, a person and even an object can be haunted as well. There are many modern homes around El Reno that have stories of paranormal activity attached to them.

One such account took place in an older home just off North Evans Street. The home was built around the 1930s and was not in the best of shape during the time of the event. The family who was renting the home at the time has shared some of their experiences with me. I visited the home on three separate occasions to take care of an older lady who was a home health patient of mine. During those visits, she told me about some of the home's dark and mysterious past.

Not long after the family moved in, they noticed that something was not quite right about their new home. It was a very rundown house, and they could tell that the owners had no intention of ever putting any money into fixing it up. The walls were lined with dark, old wood paneling that made the inside of the home feel dim and gloomy as well. The carpet was matted and worn through in several places, showing through to the floors below. Flies were abundant in the home as well as other various types of crawling insects. Due to my patient's declining health, it was difficult for her to keep the house clean, if one could even attempt to keep that decrepit house clean. Cobwebs were present throughout the house as well various water stains and mold spots caused by years of water damage. If the condition of the home wasn't scary enough, it's history would certainly dissuade anyone from ever wanting to move in.

The family started hearing strange sounds that could not be explained. They heard scratching on the walls, which could be explained by a rodent possibly taking up residence in the old home, but along with the scratching came other strange noises. Moans and crying could be heard throughout the night as well as a strange tapping noise. These noises were mainly experienced in the far back bedroom, but they had also been experienced in the living room area and the front bedroom from time to time. The family claimed that various objects would go missing only to show up weeks later in the same spot they had disappeared from. They also reported that a dark shadow, standing about six feet tall, was noted on several occasions quickly passing through a room or by a doorway. On two separate occasions, my patient witnessed her name being called out when she was alone in the house. The activity started to increase the longer they lived there, but since they were on a fixed income and not able to move, the family lived in fear for five months.

The activity reached the breaking point for my patient when she was physically attacked by the dark entity in the home. She said she was sitting up in her recliner one day, simply watching TV, when she suddenly got a very uncomfortable feeling. The room became dark despite it being a warm summer day, and she felt a heaviness settling on her chest. She said she found it hard to breath and felt something tightening around her neck. The next day, my patient moved out of her home and went to stay with her son. Her daughter and granddaughter moved out the following week.

Before leaving the home, her granddaughter went to talk to a few of the neighbors to see if she could find out any of the home's history. She was told that the house had been empty for many years prior to their moving in, but there was a rumor that years ago, one of the girls who lived in the home had practiced Satanism and committed suicide in her room, which was located at the back of the house. The family said they had not been back since.

Haunted El Reno

Whitney's Houses

Home is supposed to be the place where you feel the most comfortable. My family moved to El Reno when I was in fifth grade. Little did I know that both of the homes we lived in wouldn't be my comfort zone. Little did I know that much of my days would be spent wondering about what would happen next.

The first home we lived in was in an unassuming neighborhood. It was a rather plain house, on a block full of other plain homes. It took a while for me to notice that things weren't right there. It started out just as an uncomfortable feeling, like I was being watched. You know, the feeling you get at nighttime when your family is asleep and the whole house is dark, but you must go to bathroom, so you run as quickly as possible before the "whatever" gets you? I spent a lot of nights speed-walking through the hallway, staring only at the floor until I could get the bathroom light on. I frequently slept with the covers over my head, just in case I might catch a glimpse of something that wasn't actually there. It wasn't until a little later that my siblings and I started having more notable experiences.

At some point while living at this first house, we got a dog named Buster. He seemed to be a mix of a dachshund and a chihuahua, with a personality that definitely favored a dachshund. He was very chill, but after a few months, he started growling at unseen things in the house. Occasionally, I would go into the kitchen and he would be standing at the refrigerator, hair standing up, teeth bared and growling, like there was an invisible barrier at those moments that he refused to cross. He did this only a few times, and, aside from being slightly uncomfortable, I ignored most of these instances. However, there was one night that was a little bit different. It was late, probably around midnight, and I got out of bed to get a drink. Buster trailed behind me until he stopped as if something had hit him at the invisible threshold by the fridge. This time, he barked at me not to cross it; the hair on his back stood straight up, he had his hackles up and he just stood there, growling at something unseen. Despite his protests, I walked over to the kitchen sink, and as I grabbed a cup from the cabinet to the right of the sink, I noticed something in the backyard. As my eyes adjusted to looking out past the dim back porch light, I realized it was a lot of somethings! Lined across our back fence was a group of dogs. There were dozens of them, of all different types and colors, just sitting along the fence, staring into that kitchen window. I blinked a few times, but they didn't go away. I was frozen in front of the kitchen sink. I remember thinking to myself, "I'm losing my mind." I had prior experiences but never something so weird. I'm not exactly sure what snapped me out of the daze I was in staring out that window, but perhaps it was Buster's growling. As I hastily walked back to bed, those dogs were still there, so I, of course, covered my face.

Shortly after I turned thirteen and obtained my babysitting certificate, which I was really excited about, my parents started to leave me at home with the kids for short periods of time. I was fine with this until one evening when my sister came into my room to ask me who all the people were in the living room. I followed her into the front room, and nobody was there. She did this several times throughout the night. One day after school, my brother and sister came running frantically into my bedroom yelling that someone was trying to get in the front door. I ran out, and sure enough, the door handle was turning and jiggling violently like someone was trying to bust the door in. I won't lie—I was terrified that someone was about to burst through that door when I knew that my parents weren't due to be home for another hour or so. I ushered my siblings to the hallway and tiptoed to the front window to peak through the curtain and see who was on the porch. As I peered through the curtain, the doorknob stopped moving, and I was shocked to see that, in fact, no one was on the porch. No one was near the porch, or in the yard, or walking down the street. There was no explanation that I could have given to my brother and sister that would have put their minds at ease. Staying at home alone was no longer a novelty after that incident.

The last memorable incident at the first house we lived in occurred while we were playing outside. My sister and some neighborhood kids were playing hide and seek. As she hid by the side of the house, she said she saw a manhole cover be lifted from underneath by a dark figure with red eyes that peered out at her. At the time, she would've been around seven years old, so the experience could be explained by an overactive imagination. No one can say for sure, but it wasn't too long after that incident that we moved. Little did we know what we were in for.

The second house we lived in was just north of the El Reno cemetery. The house had white wooden siding that had seen its fair share of Oklahoma weather and a detached garage with a car port off to the side, and it sat just west of a large horse pasture. Built in the 1920s, it was a farmhouse that had been moved from its original location to where it sat when we moved in. The inside was somewhat of a maze. As you walked in the front door, you were in the living room with the dining room to the right, and you could see into the kitchen through a passthrough window with a small bar. A little farther into the house was a hallway that ran north to south. This hallway led to a door on the left that opened into another hallway, and if you kept walking north, it led to the main bathroom on the left, a dining room door on the right and a kitchen at its end. The kitchen was a somewhat small galley style with a window on the east end and door into the laundry room on the west end. Through the laundry area, there was a back door that led to the small backyard, the basement and a very narrow passageway that ran east and west to a tiny room that was referred to as the canning room. The passage to the canning room was so narrow that my siblings and I were the only ones able to get through it. There was another door to the backyard in the canning room, but it was sealed shut.

The canning room ran parallel to what would end up being my brother's room. From the first time we walked through the house, my brother's room gave me the creeps. The smell in the closet was awful, like an animal had been rotting under the floor. Directly outside my brother's room was the third hallway. This hallway was attached to a second bathroom and three bedrooms. The bedroom my sister and I shared was right in the middle of the house on the west side. It was directly across from the back bathroom and our parents' room just south of it. As I said, this house was a maze, but the general layout will help as I tell about our experiences here.

At first, the house seemed to be perfect. Aside from the creepy vibe I got from the canning room, my brother's room and the smell in his closet, everything seemed normal. First, we tried to get rid of the smell from my brother's closet. My dad checked the crawlspace underneath the house, and we had the carpets shampooed several times, but we never could get rid of that smell. I'm not sure what made my brother's room creepy. Perhaps it was the fact that it was connected to the canning room, which seemed odd all on its own, especially with its super narrow passageway. It wasn't too long after we moved in that my brother started having night terrors. It was an almost nightly occurrence that lasted for years. At first, we didn't think much of it and brushed it off as a kid thing, but then he started to sleepwalk.

After my other family members started to experience things in the house, I got curious. During many of my brother's episodes, I went into his room to ask him what was wrong. In his state of not awake, but not quite asleep, he would talk about someone named Johnny. He would say that this Johnny person was chasing him or standing outside his window, tormenting him. His episodes would last anywhere from just a few minutes to half an hour or more before he would be calm enough to go back to sleep. He never remembered those conversations. It wasn't too long before I started having nightmares, or visions if you will, myself. I would frequently be lying in bed, trying to go to sleep, when I would have flashes of things standing outside my window, just staring, wanting to get in.

The sound of footsteps in the two back hallways were also commonplace at nighttime. The back bathroom was hardly ever used, as it was always just off-putting; it was always colder in there than it was anywhere else in the house. Banging noises from the closets in my room and my brother's room were so frequent that when our cousins and friends visited, they insisted that we sleep on pallets in the living room.

When I was about fifteen, my best friend moved in with us. Shortly after she moved in, we were eating snacks and doing chores in the kitchen after school when we heard the loud slamming of a door and glass rattling. The sound was close to us, but we knew that it was not the door to the back porch or the doors to laundry room since we were standing next to those. The noise had to have come from the canning room. But that's impossible, right? That door was sealed shut. We immediately went out to the laundry area and checked that the back door was locked. We then peered through the narrow passage to the canning room. Once we saw nothing there, and we knew that nobody was in the house but us, we quickly retreated to the living room and made sure that every door was locked up tight. When my parents arrived home, my dad checked the outside of the canning room door, and we checked the inside. There was no way that thing had opened. It was sealed tight.

While my friend stayed with us, my sister used the back hallway as her bedroom since it was a pretty big hallway. She hated it, of course, as it was never short of the sound of footsteps and shuffling around at night. During one night in particular, she woke to see a woman in a colonial dress standing at the end of her bed, peering down at her. She didn't say anything—she didn't move—she just stared. Knowing that my parents' response would be, "It's just your imagination," she covered her head and waited for sleep to come.

One afternoon, as I was in the living room, my sister was in the kitchen, my brother was in his room, my dad was in his room and my mom was still at work, a mirror flew off the wall. It landed and broke about three feet from where it had been hanging on the wall for years. My dad came bounding from his room and asked what had happened. He later tried to give some explanation about how the nail had slipped, but this mirror didn't just fall straight down and bounce, it flew sideways toward the kitchen where my sister was loading the dishwasher. Besides, the nail was still hanging there as it always had been. On two occasions, while brushing my teeth in the front bathroom, which sits just next to where this mirror hung, unexplainable things happened. Once, the water came on by itself, and during another incident, the blow dryer came on by itself, despite not having been used.

   Just before my friend moved out, she and another friend were over at the house for Halloween. We were, of course, watching run-of-the-mill, spooky Halloween movies while my parents were out trick-or-treating with the younger kids, when suddenly, it felt like there was a massive atmospheric change. The air got heavy and almost felt charged. All three of us felt it, and we sat and stared at one another. One of my friends and I sat there, staring into the kitchen at some unseen force that we were all feeling, as a black mass swept across the passthrough window in the kitchen. The two of us jumped up in disbelief, said some words that our parents probably wouldn't have been too proud of and bolted to the front door. Our friend who didn't see it, just like a character in the horror movies we were watching, headed down the hallway toward the kitchen, thinking we were just trying to scare her. We, of course, were trying to talk her out of going in there, but she was out to prove that we were being jerks. We reluctantly followed. As she got to the kitchen, we heard her say, "Oh my God!" We peered in as she shoved past the two of us. All of the kitchen cabinets had been opened. At that point, we all relocated to the front porch where we waited until our parents arrived home from trick-or-treating. Our parents laughed it off and said that we had just spooked ourselves by watching scary movies. We never talked about that experience again.

   One of my most notable experiences occurred when I was seventeen. A family friend and her three-year-old daughter were staying with us for a short period of time. They shared a room with me since I had a trundle bed. It was late, probably eleven o'clock, and we were all lying down. I was on the trundle and Trish was on the twin bed, and we were watching *Freddy vs Jason* on VHS. Now, I like Freddy alright, but this movie was just silly. About halfway through, as we laid there making fun of the cheesiness, the TV turned off and the VCR ejected the movie. We both, of course, accused each other until we saw the remotes sitting out of both of our reaches on the desk. At that point, I moved onto the twin bed with Trish. As we sat there trying to rationalize what had just happened, there was loud bang from my closet, like a bowling ball had been dropped on the wood floor. We both screamed as my phone rang. It was my parents from the room next door telling us we should be asleep and that it was ridiculous that were making so much noise. After trying to explain that it wasn't us and that we were, in fact, terrified, they hung up, and we were left trying to figure out what had just happened. After what seemed like the longest night ever, we woke in the daylight and immediately sought to figure out which closet the noise had originated from. However, nothing was out of place, nothing had fallen, no clothes were disturbed and there were absolutely no clues as to what could've made that large of a bang.

I was eighteen when my parents decided to move back to the city, and we looked at several houses before finding one that was good fit. After paying the deposit, my mom and I were walking through the house, trying to decide on paint colors when she said, "Pray with me that whatever is in that El Reno house can't follow us here." I don't know if there could have been a forklift powerful enough to lift my jaw off the floor, and she knew it. After all of the times she had said, "It's just your imagination," I finally had a little bit of validation. My parents had experiences there as well, and most of them involved footsteps, noises, feelings and the occasional item disappearing only to show back up later. I'm not sure exactly what or who was in that house, but I can say that I was glad to leave it.

Tanya's Ghostly Encounter

I am often asked if I ever get scared going into some of the places investigate. When I first started paranormal investigating, there were several times that I felt uneasy and even a little spooked, but since I've been in the field for some time now, I've gotten pretty accustomed to it, and nothing really scares me anymore. In fact, I think living people can be much scarier than ghosts. Just look at all the crime we have today: the mass shootings, serial killers, politics. But seriously, even sending your child to school can be frightening. Still, I often get asked if I get scared during the investigations, and the only one that really comes to mind took place before one of our investigations even began.

Our team had been called out to investigate one of the older homes in El Reno. The house had served many purposes over the years, including as a small café where they served fried chicken and bar-b-que to many of the railroad workers during the early years of the town. The house had been investigated years before, so this place had a history of hauntings, but this time, things were different. The family that was currently living in the house felt threatened in their home. The children were waking up to shadow figures standing over their beds, and no one felt safe. The owners of the home reported that their oldest son spent a lot of time alone in his room, which was in basement area. The basement had been converted into a living area with bunk beds, a couch and a bathroom. He would spend several days on the couch without eating or sleeping; he would just stare off into the darkness. Their son had been in the military and had seen action while overseas, and he suffered from severe PTSD because of it. With his change in behavior, and the clients afraid to be in their own home, we decided to make the house an urgent case and scheduled an appointment for a walk-through and an interview. Little did I know just how much this investigation was going to affect me.

On the night before the investigation, I was up late. I've always been kind of a night owl, which means sleep doesn't come easily for me. I had been up late watching TV, and my husband had already gone to bed. The kids were staying with my mom that night, so I decided to sleep on the couch that night so that I wouldn't disturb my husband. Due to my work as a night nurse for many years, it is hard for me to sleep in a dark room, so I also decided to leave one of the kitchen lights on. Not long after I closed my eyes, I noticed a change in the darkness of the room. I opened my eyes and noticed the kitchen light was off. I figured that my husband had come in and turned it off, since he does that quite often, so I got up and turned the light back on. I lay back down, and as soon as I closed my eyes, the light was off again. I got back up, walked back into the kitchen, and turned the light back on. As I was lying back down on the couch, I realized that I had never heard my husband get up or enter the living room area. In fact, I could hear him snoring in the bedroom. I suddenly felt my shoulders being forcefully pushed deeper into the couch. Panic took over as I tried to get up. I could move my arms but not enough to get up. I tried banging on the wall to get my husband's attention, but I couldn't get my arms up high enough. I tried to say the Lord's prayer, but I couldn't speak, so I just tried to say it in my mind. I couldn't seem to get through the words despite knowing it since I was a young child. After about five attempts, I was finally able to recite the Lord's prayer from beginning to end. Once the prayer was finished, the entity released me.

I sat up quickly, and my heart felt as if it was about to jump out of my chest. I looked over to my front door and standing in the doorway was a dark figure that was almost six feet tall. I told him he wasn't allowed in my home, and he was gone. Afterward, I went through my house turning on every light. I couldn't fall asleep after that. When my husband got ready to leave for work at six o'clock the next morning, I asked him not to go. He told me he couldn't miss work, so I stayed up, alone in the house, with all the lights still on. When it was almost time to get ready to go to the client's house for the walk-through, I called one of my team members to tell them that I wasn't going to be able to make it that day. I explained to her what had happened to me during the night, and I was so tired that I was afraid I'd fall asleep behind the wheel. She told me I had to go and that she would be by to pick me up soon.

Later, we arrived at the client's home and made introductions. We started to head into the house when I stopped in the doorway. I looked over to the client and asked where the basement was. She showed me to the doorway, and I descended the stairs. As I reached the bottom of the stairs, I glanced over to another set of stairs that once led out to the side of the house. Sitting on the staircase was the same dark entity I had seen in my home then night before, the one that had held me down. There was such a darkness about him that was pure evil. My fear turned to anger as I realized that this spirit, this negative form or energy, had come to my home to try to keep me from coming out that day. We finished conducting our interview and scheduled our investigation for that weekend.

We set our equipment up around the home, which included several nighttime cameras in the basement area as well as in the children's room. We started our first session in the basement where most of the activity had taken place. I was sitting on the couch with another investigator when I noticed some movement on the floor. I looked down and saw a dark shadow crawling there. Its skin appeared charred and the only color I could see was coming from the whites of its eyes. During that time, another investigator said he was smelling smoke, like something was burning. Images started to fill my head like a movie was playing out right before my eyes. I could see an army convoy traveling down a dusty road. One of the Humvees was struck by a mortar shell causing it to overturn, and I could see the soldiers burning inside. I went upstairs and asked the father to call his son and ask him if he had a friend named Paul that was stationed with him overseas. I then told him to ask his son how he had died. As it turns out, the son did have a friend that he had lost while he was serving. He had burned to death in a Humvee after it was struck by artillery. The son's friend, however, was not the evil presence in the house. I believe his friend was there to protect him from the evil presence. He was positioned between the couch and the stairway where the dark entity liked to stay. We were able to gather several other pieces of evidence that night, and we did a cleansing of the home with sage and prayer. When we followed up with the client, they reported that they felt much more at ease in the home and that no other incidents had occurred.

Other Hauntings in El Reno Homes

Another story that has been given to us came from a young lady who lived in a haunted house in El Reno from 1990 to 1996. She lived in a home near Woodson and Shepard, and she and her sister shared a room with a set of bunk beds in it. As a young girl, the first full-body apparition she saw was that of a little, fair-skinned girl in a white dress with red, curly hair. One night when she was older, she and her sister were both woken up by their bunk beds shaking violently. Their grandmother came running down the hall and told the girls to go to her room where she took out her Bible and started to pray. After a while, the shaking stopped. The girl's grandmother started having dreams of babies hanging from the trees in the backyard. One night, on one of the walls in the room where the girls slept, a black, greasy handprint of a small child appeared. No matter how much they scrubbed, it never came off.

Soon, their family started to experience more paranormal activity. The girl said they would be sitting in the living room watching TV when they would hear the refrigerator door open and close. These experiences had gotten so bad that the family had the home blessed. They were told by a psychic medium that there was a man in the garage who wouldn't leave. The psychic told the spirit that it was fine for him to stay there as long as he didn't harm the family in any way. A few years later, one of the girl's friends was dropping her off at home when he asked if she lived there. She said that she did, and he replied, "You know that house is haunted right? I used to live there and the people that use to live there before me told me that a guy hung himself in the garage." Chills ran down her spine. That explained why the spirit was haunting the garage, but to this day, there is no answer as to why there were children haunting her childhood home.

We also found another story that was shared on a public website. It said that a couple had just bought their first home in 1996 in El Reno. They knew that someone had passed away in the home but didn't think too much of it. One night, the husband woke up and saw the profile of a man standing next to his bed. He could make out every detail of his face and clothes despite the fact that the room was so dark. At first, he thought he was dreaming. He tried to close his eyes and open them again, but the man was still standing there. The husband said that the man had a sharp, hawk-like nose, a gray beard lining his jaw and a bald head on top with his hair circling just above his ears. The husband also said that the man was wearing old-fashioned, thick-framed, round glasses and a monk's robe with a hood down the back.

Haunted El Reno

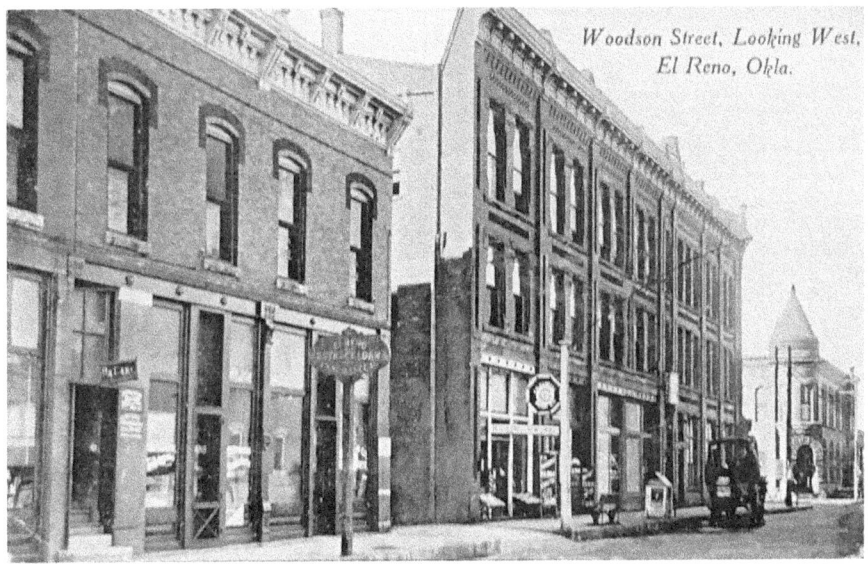

Woodson Street, 1918. *Tommy Neathery.*

The husband said he stared at him for several minutes, then closed his eyes and went to sleep.

A year or so later, the husband had another ghostly encounter. He said he was sitting on the couch watching TV when he noticed a swirling blue smoke or mist forming about five feet away. He said he clenched his eyes shut and opened them again to see if it was simply his eyes playing tricks on him, but the mist was still there. The mist continued to linger there for a few more minutes before it simply faded away.

The husband was not the only one seeing strange things in the home. One of his daughters said she woke up one night and saw Jesus standing in her closet. None of the accounts of the ghostly apparitions from his family fit the description of the lady who had passed away in the bathtub from a brain aneurism, but it left the husband wondering if her death had somehow created a portal for spirits to come through from the other side.

Two of the stories that we have collected seem be about the same spirit haunting two different locations that are only half a mile away from each other. The first story takes place in a home where a woman, her fiancé and her four children lived. She said that her son had gotten up in the middle of the night and thought he saw his little sister playing with some of her new toys. However, when he looked toward the beds, he saw that both of his sisters were asleep. The woman's son said that the little girl had long, black hair that covered half of her face and was wearing a white dress. He said he became so scared that he ran to his own bed and didn't get up again until the next morning. After that incident, they all started to see her. The mom stated that she was taking a shower one night when she felt someone touch her back. She said she thought it was her fiancé playing a trick on her but realized that he wasn't in the bathroom. She was starting to think that perhaps it was the shower curtain when it happened again. She yelled out for her fiancé to come in. She was so scared by the experience that she made her fiancé stay the bathroom while she finished her shower.

The second story takes place in a home not far from that of the first incident. Another woman also claimed that she saw the girl in her home. She said she was relaxing on her bed when she heard a furious knocking coming from her closet. Suddenly, she saw a young girl in a white dress with long, black hair standing in the middle of the room, staring at her. She just stood there, staring at the woman for several minutes. The woman said she started to hyperventilate, and then the girl just vanished. The activity didn't end there. After that first incident, the woman claimed that her bedroom door would slam in her face and that she never felt alone in her room. The woman later found out that years before, there had been a terrible fire at the house when it was being used as a salon. While they were doing renovations, they found a huge pit in the ground beneath the house that was filled with ashes. She never wanted to go back to the house again.

This next story was given to us by a lady who wishes to remain anonymous since she currently still lives in the home that this story is about, so for our purposes, we will call her Jane. Jane and her family moved into a historic home in El Reno around 1999. The home was built in the late 1800s; it's an old, two-story brick home that some refer to as "the mansion," despite that the fact that it is not one. At one point, the home had been converted into apartments, and other additions have been made over the years. When Jane and her family bought the house, they renovated it and turned it back into a single-family home. During the renovation, Jane noticed something odd about the plaster inside the walls, which they had to knock it out to replace it with drywall. The plaster contained black hairs throughout the mix. Jane's family knew that the previous owner had also had the house blessed, but they never asked why. They would find out soon enough.

One night, Jane said she and her husband were sitting on the couch watching TV when she spotted something near the dining room. She asked her husband if the dog was outside; he said she was and asked why. She told him she saw something small, around three feet tall, and brown standing in the dining room area. He said he had seen the same thing. They both jumped up and went to look, even opening the closet door, but nothing was there.

Jane said another innocent happened while she was in the restroom. She claimed that the toilet paper rolls started to spin very quickly, rolling the paper off into the trash. She called out to her husband, but when he walked in, it suddenly stopped. He tried to explain the incident away by stating that it was most likely the heater or vent that caused the toilet paper to spin, because there was no way anyone could spin it that fast by hand. Suddenly, the toilet paper started to spin again. Jane said her daughter will not go to the restroom alone in the house despite having lived there all her life; she always makes the family dog go with her. Jane said her daughter is also afraid to go down the hall or to her room unless someone is with her.

Jane said that other things have occurred in the house over the years, but one other encounter that really stood out to me took place while Jane was in the kitchen cooking dinner. In the hall, next to the kitchen, there is a full-length mirror. Jane said she once looked over toward the mirror and saw her son standing there in the same white T-shirt he typically wears. She said she called out to him to tell him dinner was almost done, but he didn't answer. She went to his room to find him, but he was no were to be found. Who was the person peering at her through the mirror?

El Reno holds so much history in it that it's no wonder so many of its homes and businesses are haunted. Much of El Reno's past still lives on today in the bones of the old homes of El Reno.

The Canadian County Museum

The Canadian County Museum sits near the heart of El Reno on 300 South Grand. Tucked away from any major highways or roads, the buildings of El Reno's past, which were once separated by miles, now sit side by side to give visitors a small glimpse into this city's historical past.

The Canadian County Museum was chartered in October 1968 and opened its doors to the public in 1970. Jack and Patricia Reuter spent most of their lives collecting relics, which is most of what visitors see in the museum today. From Native American goods and art to an old bar top with a large mirror that was used during the original land run, the museum has plenty to offer anyone who wishes to learn a little more about Oklahoma and its history.

The museum sits on a corner lot that extends from the street up to the railroad tracks. There are eight historic buildings on the property, including the original Rock Island Railroad Depot. Built in 1907, the Rock Island Railroad connected El Reno to every corner of the United States. During World War I, soldiers traveling across the United States would often stop at the depot to purchase paper goods and other supplies from the Red Cross Canteen before leaving to serve overseas. The original building was constructed by a group of local Boy Scouts, and can still be seen on the museum's site today. However, the inside of the building is closed due to disrepair.

The Rock Island Depot had some dark days in its past. During the period of racial segregation in America, African Americans were not allowed in the same area of the building as white people. Both the drinking areas and

Red Cross canteen located at the Canadian County Museum. *Carnegie Library.*

waiting areas were separated. While the "whites" had nice benches to sit on while they waited for the train to arrive, African Americans were left to wait in the baggage claim area where luggage and various goods would be unloaded from the train. Today, that area holds a lot of memories from the railroad's past as well as a few ghostly remains from the years gone by.

If you visit the museum and walk from the baggage claim area of the Rock Island Depot toward the main ticketing area, you can pass through a walkway filled with historical pictures and cameras. Old family photos line the walls, and family photo albums that date back to the 1800s are stored behind two glass showcases. There are several types of cameras on display for anyone with a passion for photography. Cameras that were used over one hundred years ago can be found behind glass cases for everyone to enjoy. From family photos, to single portraits, the eyes of the past follow as you move on into the next rooms of the museum.

The next room you can enter is filled with the history of local doctors, along with their various pieces of equipment and supplies. From old glass

Old railroad depot. *Tommy Neathery.*

medicine bottles to a nurse's uniform, this room has just about everything to showcase from the everyday life of a doctor in the old frontier. Bone saws lie in glass cases along with syringes (the non-disposable, reusable and no safety cap kind), medicine bags, personal clothing and a doctor's exam table are just a few of the items located in this room. This room even has an old burial suit on display; it is a child's size and reusable as well. If that's not creepy enough for you, just move over to the next glass case where you can look in and see hundreds of human teeth lying about.

Dr. Jonas B. Spitler is one of the frontier physicians featured in this room. He is considered to have been the first physician to practice in the Oklahoma and Indian Territories. Dr. Spitler graduated from the University of Illinois and attended the Keokuk Medical School in Iowa before he and his family moved to the Oklahoma Territory in 1892. Soon, he began making his rounds in a horse-drawn buggy and eventually settled his family in Mustang, Oklahoma, where he is considered to be one of the town's founding fathers. Dr. Spitler was a true physician and put his heart and soul into helping people. Doctors back then didn't make a lot of money, and they often faced financial difficulties just like their neighbors. However, Dr. Spitler never refused medical care to anyone for financial reasons, and he would often cross the Canadian River to spend days tending to sick members of the Chickasaw Nation.

If you continue through the building, you can pass the old ticket seller's booth with the original window still intact, as if it were open ready to sell tickets to waiting customers. The booth leads out into a large, open area that was originally the waiting area for the depot. Solid wood benches, still sturdy and in place, are located at the front of the building. Along the waiting area's walls, you can find various artifacts, many of which are from the Native American tribes of Oklahoma. Ceremonial garments, headdresses, weapons, a buffalo head and many other items are showcased to help visitors understand a little more about the ways of Native American life as they were before Oklahoma became a state.

The Canadian County Museum reminds its visitors that frontier life was no easy task. While many people did perish, many others thrived and continued to build homes for themselves and their families on the Oklahoma plains. The museum showcases various items from Oklahoma's earliest days, including hatpins, shoes, clothing and even furniture, so that visitors can truly get a sense of what their lives may have been like over a century ago.

I investigated the museum for the first time around 2013. When we arrived, my team and I set up several cameras around the building and gathered our equipment. Our first destination was the main lobby area. As we sat quietly in the darkness, we could hear the wooden floor planks creak

Some of El Reno's first residents, late 1800s. *Tommy Neathery.*

as the old building began to settle. We strained our eyes against the darkness to see if we could detect any movement or see any shadows. We started our EVP session by asking general questions, "Is anyone here with us tonight that would like to speak with us?" The silence continued. After about thirty minutes with no activity occurring, we decided to move back to the baggage area and try our luck there. We continued the investigation by asking some more general questions and conducting a K2 sweep of the area. Since there were very few windows in the rooms, we decided we would use the FLIR (a thermal imaging camera used to pick up on temperature changes in the area), doing our best to avoid the glass in the showcases. As we were panning around the room, we noticed a change in one area. We quickly snapped a picture on the camera. Soon, we were getting responses to our questions on our voice box device. When we reviewed the picture and our audio, we discovered that we had been visiting with an elderly African American man. We never did discover who he was or why he had chosen to stay there after he had passed away. Was he attached to an object in the room, or was he perhaps an old railroad employee who was simply happy being around the things he knew best? Perhaps we may be able to unlock the mystery of the man during future investigations if he still resides at the old train depot.

Just across the drive sits one of El Reno's oldest hotels. Built in 1892 by J.M. Kemp, it was the oldest standing commercial building in El Reno. The hotel once stood at the corner of Choctaw and Wade Streets and remained in business until 1975, when it closed its doors forever. The building was later donated to the museum and moved to the site in 1984.

The building is an old, two-story, wood framed building created in a Folk Victorian style. The museum has restored the hotel as close as it possibly can to its original appearance. When you first step into the building, you are welcomed by a small living room area filled with antique chairs, an old fireplace and a check-in desk with old-fashioned cubbies and room keys. After you walk past the desk, you can ascend the narrow, steep staircase up to the rooms—just be careful not to bump your head on the low-level ceiling. People seem to have been much shorter back in those days. Once upstairs, you are met by a group of small doors lining each wall. The wooden doors that once provided privacy have since been replaced by glass windows, giving you a peek into the past of what the hotel would have looked like. You will not find a soft king-sized bed, but rather a small, cast iron bedframe with an old handsewn quilt that kept patrons warm on cold winter nights. A public bathroom was often shared by all of the guests, and depending on the time in history, this restroom could have been indoors or outdoors. Downstairs,

El Reno's first hotel. *Carnegie Library.*

guests would have taken their meals in a small dining room with an adjacent kitchen that made it easier for staff to serve food. It was in the dining room area that we decided to set up our DVR (digital video recording) system.

With several reports of people hearing footsteps and even running, we decided to set up our audio equipment throughout the hotel. The building is small and easily accessible, so we decided we would place only four of our night vision cameras throughout the building. We put two upstairs, one facing in each direction, and two downstairs, one facing into the dining room and the other facing out into the open common room and front lobby. Since we were a small team that night, we all decided to stay together to help decrease the chances of cross-contaminating our evidence with noise. We started our first EVP session in the dining room of the old hotel. We were almost an hour into the investigation, and nothing much had happened so far (which is very common for true investigations, it's not like the overdramatized TV shows). It was a very quiet evening, and despite it being Oklahoma, there was little to no wind at all that night. As we were sitting quietly downstairs, we all heard a very distinct "thump" come from right above our heads. We quickly turned to one another to see if we had all heard the noise. Soon after, we heard another loud noise. Then much to our surprise, the thumping increased, getting louder and louder, then faster and faster. Before long, it sounded as if someone or something was running back and forth along the small hallway upstairs. Two of us jumped up and started toward the staircase, and we could still hear the running as we approached the stairs. Just as we grabbed the rail to ascend, the noise stopped. When we reached the top of the stairs, no one was in sight. There was a distinct chill in the air despite the fact that it was summertime and very warm outside. We knew we were not alone. There was no sign of any animal being present, and we knew that a living person could not have been up there to make the noise. There was only one way up and one way down, and from where we were sitting, no one could have ascended the stairs without us knowing. When we pulled the footage from our camera system, we could plainly make out what appeared to be a mist form in the middle of the hall. It was small in stature, no more than four feet tall, and we could see it moving around in the hallway. We could also see it start to dissipate just before our arrival. Was this a friendly spirit simply playing a game of hide and seek, or did we scare off whatever may have been running around upstairs when we decided to search it out for ourselves? We didn't experience much more after that, and the building seemed to quiet down. Hopefully, we will be able to learn more about the ghostly footsteps of the historic El Reno hotel one day.

There are other buildings located around the property of the museum, but there is one haunted location that does not consist of wooden walls or brick and mortar. Sitting alongside the old railroad tracks, between the depot and the big red barn, is an old caboose car. You will not find a GPS system or even an old radio in it; travel back then was much different than it is today. If you were lucky enough to be able to afford the finer things in life, then you may have been able to purchase a ticket on the train. It was a much easier way to travel, and it decreased your chances of getting saddle sore. Once you purchased a ticket on the train, you could sit back and relax as you watched the beauty of the landscape pass by your window. That is, if the loud rumbling of the steel wheels on the track and the blowing of the whistle didn't bother you too much. The vibrations of the turning wheels and the swaying of train car made for long trips across open country, and travelers would often ride for days on end before reaching their destinations. Despite the sounds one would hear while traveling on a train, the travel time was much faster and more comfortable than riding on horseback. The old caboose is where employees of the railroad would have slept on long trips. Fitted with a few small bunks and pull-down seats, this small space was often a second home to them.

At the Canadian County Museum, the car is accessible for visitors to walk in and look around, but some of the paranormal activity takes place just outside it. My team and I didn't get to investigate the old caboose due to time constraints, but we did get to witness something. As we stood facing the train, several of us saw what appeared to be legs walking back and forth behind the train car, but it wasn't just one set of legs, it was two. We walked around to the other side of the caboose to see if anyone else was on the property that night. Since it was after hours, no one should have been there but us. When we walked behind it, no one was there. Just beyond the cars is a chain-link fence and past it, the railroad, so if anyone had been on the grounds, there is no way they could have run without us seeing them. We are not sure who was walking around the old train caboose that night, but we do know for certain that it wasn't someone who was still alive.

Also located on the property is the old Mennoville Mennonite Church. The building houses several pews, a pulpit and an old piano. The pulpit still stands, waiting for the pastor to preach out to his congregation. Next to the church sits an old one-room schoolhouse with a potbelly stove, a teacher's desk and several old students' desks lined up in two small rows. The large, red barn sits next to the old hotel and is filled with various items, including carriages, pictures, articles of clothing, old trunks and, my personal favorite, the solid wood bar with the original, old-time, warped mirror that was used during the original Oklahoma land run. The original Darlington Jail house sits a few feet behind the barn. It's a small building that houses two small cells, their iron bars still in place. Native Americans who didn't follow the strict rules of the territory or who refused to forget their native ways were often housed here. It is also said that the Doolin gang, also known as the Wild Bunch, spent some time in this small jail house. They were an American outlaw gang that was known for robbing stagecoaches, trains and banks across Oklahoma, Arkansas and Kansas during the 1890s. Just behind the jail sits General Sheridan's headquarters. This small log building was once located at Fort Reno and was later moved to the property as part of the museum.

This past fall, we went back to the museum to investigate after our annual paranormal conference, Paracon–Oklahoma. The following are some of the stories our group shared after investigating this site.

Martha Decker, a paranormal investigator and author from southeast Texas, shared with us the experiences she had while investigating some of the museum's buildings. These are her accounts. Most of Martha's experiences took place in the red barn. She was there with another paranormal investigator and her friend, Vickie Higdon. They were investigating with a phone app that works by attaching words to various levels of energy. While they were in the building, they got the name "Wyatt" through the equipment. They later discovered that a photograph of a man named Wyatt was hanging on the wall. While in another area of the building, the kept getting the word "soldier" and a man's last name. As they went to leave the building, they realized there was a display by the door that contained a mannequin wearing an old soldier's uniform. Next to the exhibit was an information card that was related to the uniform in some way. The name they had gotten earlier was on that very card. The women also reported feeling a cold spot and a breeze in the building when there was no source for the breeze to be found.

The women had another experience while they were in the old train depot. While standing in the hall, they received more words through the equipment: "sick" and "disease." They later realized that they were standing in the doorway to the room of medical displays when these words came through.

Another group said that they also experienced some activity in the El Reno hotel. Linda Hillard, Jeromy Jones, Pam Jones and Richard were upstairs, at the far end of the landing, using a piece of equipment called poltercom. They were asking various questions and obtaining several responses from possible spirits. They established that one of the entities was that of a male who had stayed there with his family. When they asked the spirit for his age, he responded by saying that he was forty-five. Linda then responded back, saying, "Hello, forty-five. I am sixty-two," to which the spirit replied, "Old." Richard reported that he felt the hairs on his arm stand straight up. Later, when they returned upstairs to retrieve their equipment, Jeromy yelled out, "We're back," and the poltercom responded by saying, "I see!"

Another group that was investigating the same building reported that they heard footsteps upstairs, and they saw what appeared to be a tall shadow in the figure of a person standing in the hallway.

In the old church building on the property, several people reported that they received a lot of words pertaining to religion in the building. They also said that they experienced the feeling of someone watching them. Many people reported that they also felt uneasy around the old jail area.

With all of this Oklahoma history located in one small area, how could the museum not be haunted? Whether you are interested in local history or paranormal encounters, the Canadian County Museum is well worth a visit.

Haunted Highways of El Reno

Dead Man's Curve

It seems like every town has a legend about a cry baby bridge or a dead man's curve, and El Reno is no different. What I find so interesting is that when you do an internet search of haunted locations in El Reno, not many stories come up. You won't find many stories talking about the Centre Theater or the Canadian County Museum on many websites, but I did come across one story several times that was about a dead man's curve. The road is located just behind the old sewage plant, which was built in 1941 and now sits abandoned. Its building is heap of metal sitting in decay, with broken windows and brick and mortar that have fallen to the ground. This location not only possesses an eerie beauty about it, but it also presents danger to anyone who may think about trespassing on the site.

The road is a small, two-lane road located in the backcountry of El Reno. I have found several versions of what may have occurred on the road. One version says that a man tried to take the curve too fast while driving a van filled with nineteen people. The story says that he lost control of the vehicle, causing a wreck that killed all nineteen passengers. Another version of the story states that the van only had nine passengers in it when it was wrecked. Locals say that if you park along that road on a quiet night, you can still hear the screeching of the tires and the grinding of the metal as the vehicle is torn apart. They also say that you can hear the screaming of the victims as they lay dying along the roadside.

Whether the story is mere legend or true, the fact remains that the road is very dangerous, and many accidents have occurred on the site. Should you try to seek out the legend and hear the blood-curdling screams of its victims, take caution, you never know what or who you may see along the road.

The Hunchback of Route 66

There is second legend that surrounds another road in El Reno. It is a well-known highway that was once used as a main road to lead travelers across the United States. Route 66, established on November 11, 1926, stretched for 2,448 miles, extending from Chicago, Illinois, to Santa Monica, California. The highway was one of the main thoroughfares used during the dust bowl of the 1930s, when families had to find their way to California in search of better lives. It later became very a popular vacation route for those who wished to have a scenic drive across America, and it is still used for that today. Also known as the "Mother road," this popular highway inspired the legendary song "Get Your Kicks on Route 66." The song was first produced by Capital Records in 1946 and was performed by several artists, including Nat King Cole and Chuck Berry. This stretch of highway also inspired a hit TV show called *Route 66*, which was about two American drifters traveling along the famous route. The show first aired in 1960 and would last for another four years, receiving a few Emmy nominations. The most noted Emmy nomination would be to a guest star on the show, Ethel Waters, who was the first African American actress to receive an Emmy nomination.

On a long patch of Route 66, between El Reno and Weatherford, there is a legend of a hunchback man. Many people have claimed to see the man, and some have even claimed that they gave him a ride, but no one seems to know where he came from or why he chose to walk along this lonely stretch of highway. It is said that he is often seen wandering the road on rainy or cloudy nights. Witnesses say he wears a long, brown trench coat with a Bogie-style hat pulled down over his eyes to help shield his face from the rain. One unlucky driver said that he ran into the Hunchback one night, literally. She said that she and her son were driving down the highway when she saw the man directly in front of her car. She tried to swerve, but she was too late. She said she felt the impact of the car hitting him and immediately pulled over to check on the victim. However, when she got out of the car, she could find no trace of him or any damage to the car.

Another driver reported that he was driving along the road when he came upon a man walking in the rain with his brown coat pulled tightly around him. The driver said he stopped and offered the man a ride. He states that he drove with the man for a while, sharing his love of God and witnessing to him, when suddenly, the man was gone without a trace. Another driver claimed that he also picked up the wandering stranger on a wet, rainy night. He claimed his passenger was an old, eerie man who never spoke a word to him. The driver said the passenger suddenly grabbed for the door handle and attempted to jump out, so he quickly pulled over, but the man had already disappeared. He thought the man was gone until he passed him once again a few miles down the road.

Did the man in the trench coat originally pass away after being hit by a car so many years ago? Does he continue to relive that same tragic night from so many years ago? Should you ever find yourself driving down this stretch of Route 66 on a cold, rainy night, you might want to keep your eyes open. You never know who you might run into on the road, and perhaps you to will see the famous Hunchback of Route 66.

Ghostly Route 66

There is another story that takes place on the old Route 66 between Yukon and El Reno. Several drivers have witnessed the same ghostly encounter with a man in the middle of the road. One summer night, while driving down the highway, a witness claimed they saw a mist develop in the middle of the road. It was around July, and the air was dry due to a drought. The closer the witness got to the mist, the more it started to form into the outline of a man, but the mist disappeared as she drove through it. The witness later told the story to one of her friends who said it reminded her of a tale of an old Native American man who was hit by a car after passing out drunk in the middle of the road. This witness wasn't the only one to have witnessed this ghostly encounter. Similar stories have emerged from various people who encountered the same ghostly apparition. One person states that they even got out of their car in search of a body because they believed they had hit someone. So, if you're out driving on a hot summer night along Route 66, keep an eye out for the ghost and be careful of where you drive.

Haunted El Reno

Foreman Road—Between Yukon and El Reno

Foreman Road is a two-lane, unmarked backroad that stretches from Eleventh Street in Yukon to Route 66, where it merges to west of town in El Reno. During my high school years, Foreman Road was considered the "back way" to get to Oklahoma City. I think this was the way my parents preferred to send me to the city because it kept me from driving on the highway. By day, which is when I preferred to drive that way, you can the old farmhouses, great, old grain silos and wide expanses of farmland that line the road. By night, however, the road has a definite creepy factor. The street lights are scarce if not nonexistent once you pass the short grouping of homes and the elementary school just east of Shepherd heading toward Yukon, so most of the road is in complete darkness.

On three occasions, as I was making the night trip to Oklahoma City, there were strange occurrences. The first incident happened while I was driving my 1985 Ford Mustang GL. It was a quiet night at the end of winter, so it was still cold outside. The trees that lined the side of the road looked like skeletons without their leaves, and the cloud cover limited the moonlight that usually shone onto the open fields. As I came to a narrow bridge over a small creek in a wooded area, my radio started to skip around with intermittent static. Annoyed, I turned it off, and a few short seconds later, I lost all of my lights. My dash lights, radio and headlights were all suddenly off. A little startled that something was wrong with my car, I slowly moved to pull over. As I was slowing, all lights came back on as quickly as they had gone off, and there were no more issues for the rest of the drive. I mentioned the incident to my parents, at which point they checked the obvious: fuses, battery (which was new) and alternator. They were all in working order.

The second incident occurred in the middle of summer. I had wrecked my Mustang, so I was driving a Chevrolet Cavalier Z24 convertible. I had made the trek from El Reno to Yukon down Foreman Road several times after the first incident with no issue, so I thought nothing of it. I only had the normal, eerie feeling that I always got while I was on that road at night. This time, I was not listening to the radio, and the moon was full and bright, reflecting off the crops in the fields on either side of me. As I reached the bridge, the feeling of being watched swept over me, and I lost all of my lights. "Okay, this is weird," I thought. Again, just as before, as I slowed to stop, the lights came back on. I was a little shaken up this time, but there was no further incident.

The third instance occurred just before I moved away from El Reno. This time, I was driving a newer Nissan Altima on my way to work in Yukon. For the third time, in the same location, I lost all the lights in the car, only for them to turn back on and function without error for the rest of the trip. I moved away from El Reno in 2006, so my trips on Foreman Road were few and far between after that. I mostly pushed my experiences to the back of my mind. After all, I'd never heard anyone else talk about similar stories. Everyone just talked about the eerie vibes of the road at night.

It wasn't until I spoke with a friend, Cara Pershall, an Oklahoma native, while researching for this book that I found someone who had shared a similar experience. Cara had also lived El Reno for a time and spoke of two teens that had lost their lives in a car accident around an s-curve that was just a little west of my experiences. She said she had heard travelers report seeing apparitions of the wandering teens and had seen them herself. The electrical disruptions and radio interference, however, are reported just east of the s-curve near the narrow bridge, which Cara said she had also experienced on numerous occasions.

It's been a while since I have driven down Foreman at night, but during the day, it looks much like it did twelve years ago when I used it regularly. Is there a ghostly presence causing the car disruptions? Could it be explained by some natural source in the area? I'm not sure we'll ever get an answer to those questions, but I can say that nowadays, I take the highway.

Fort Reno

As you exit Highway 81 and pass through the gates toward the fort, you are met by open fields that stretch on for mile after mile. Cattle graze nearby, and you may be lucky enough to see a large red-tailed hawk swoop down to catch its next lunch. It's a rather peaceful place now, much different than what it must have been like so many years ago. From horse and buggy to military transport, Fort Reno has seen many people come and go through its gates over the past 143 years. In 1874, Fort Reno was established as a temporary military camp to protect the Cheyenne-Arapaho Agency at Darlington. The camp functioned as the Fifth Infantry and Sixth Cavalry soldiers' "Camp Near the Cheyenne Agency" for nineteen months until it was expanded upon and named as a fort. In February 1876, General Philip Sheridan named the permanent military post Fort Reno to honor his close friend, Major General Jesse L. Reno of Virginia, who had been killed during the Civil War in 1863. Sheridan's headquarters, a small log cabin structure, now sits on the property of the Canadian County Historical Museum in El Reno.

Soldiers at the fort, including those in cavalry and infantry units, the Buffalo soldiers, Cheyenne and Arapaho Indian scouts and U.S. Marshals, were charged with policing the area of the unassigned lands prior to the land runs. During that time, many "Boomers" tried to sneak into the area and stake claim to the best lands prior to the actual opening. While the only battle near the fort was the Battle of Sand Hill in 1875, from 1892 to 1908, troops from Fort Reno were utilized in political disputes, including the Spanish-

American War in Cuba and rebellions among the Native Americans, in addition to the roles they had during the land runs.

In 1908, the fort was closed as an active military base and reactivated by the U.S. Army as a remount station, or a training ground for mules and horses that were to be used in military service. Under the leadership of Majors Daniels and Weeks, along with Captain Hardeman, the fort was refurbished and expanded. Soon, the fields were filled with military horses and mules that would be used during both world wars and Korea. Trained horses and mules were also shipped to other countries to be used by the Allied forces, and they were often accompanied by Fort Reno remount troops. The fort's grounds were also home to polo competitions, horse races, shows, auctions and other community activities. Following the end of World War II, in 1948, Fort Reno was closed and turned over to the USDA. It has since been the home of the USDA Grazinglands Research Laboratory and the Visitor's Center and Museum.

The Visitors' Center and Museum is a remodeled officer's quarters that hosts hundreds of visitors each year. This two-story building is now the home of historical photos, service uniforms and weapons from the fort's functioning days. Visitors and staff have reported feeling watched while in the building. If you stay long enough, you may even hear the chatter of long-lost voices or the footsteps of an unseen visitor. Patrons have even reported feeling as if their hair had been pulled as they toured the artifacts.

Located three miles west and two miles north of present-day El Reno, the Visitor's Center and Museum, the Cavalry Museum, the chapel and the Fort Reno Cemetery are all open for public touring. Other structures on the property include the officer's quarters, a Victorian-style home, a commissary and armory and a barn. Considering Fort Reno's history, it's no surprise that stories of unconventional visitors have arisen over the years—visitors whose names you won't find in a guest registration book but might see on a tombstone in the fort's cemetery.

The Welcome Center at Fort Reno

The first building you come to after driving down the fort's long entry road is the Welcome Center, and it is here that you will check in. Built in 1936 as an officer's quarters, the Welcome Center is a small, whitewashed building with a covered porch. When you first enter the building, you are greeted

Fort Reno's officers' quarters, currently known as the Welcome Center. *Tanya McCoy.*

by a small, open reception area with a glass case full of small souvenirs. Lining the walls are various books and goods that are available to purchase for anyone who wishes to learn a bit of history. There is also a room in the building's basement where you can find a large, round table piled high with books and photo albums that are open and ready to share some of Fort Reno's past.

To the left of the entryway, there is a beautiful wooden staircase that leads up to the second floor. At the top of the winding staircase, there is a very narrow hallway full of old rooms. Wooden floors line all the rooms, and the creaking of the wood echoes throughout the building as you pass from one room to the next. Various artifacts are displayed throughout the building,

Indian scouts at Fort Reno. *Tommy Neathery.*

from officer's boots to uniforms and even bunks. They allow visitors to see how the officers would have lived from day to day in the building.

Jim Johnston has volunteered on and off at the fort since 1989. As a current member of the fort's board, Jim spends his Tuesdays in the Welcome Center, so I asked him about the reports of paranormal activity in the building. I had heard of various encounters over the years from eyewitnesses, and I was curious to know if Jim himself had had any experiences. He shared a few stories with me about experiences he had been witness to throughout the other buildings around the fort. One of his stories came from a visitor, who claimed that while she was walking around the building, looking at all the artifacts, she suddenly felt a forceful tug on her head. As she turned to see who had touched her, there was no one to be seen. She quickly ran downstairs to report what had happened to Jim.

There have been other reports of the sounds of someone walking upstairs in heavy boots. Cold spots have also been reported throughout

Officers' quarters building at Fort Reno. *Tanya McCoy.*

the building, and many people report the feeling of being watched. Many believe that the building is still haunted by a lieutenant colonel who supposedly committed suicide in the upstairs bathroom by shooting himself in the head. One story even stated that repairs had to be made to patch the bullet hole in the ceiling.

Do soldiers still walk the narrow halls of the Welcome Center and pull the hair of unsuspecting visitors? Perhaps you yourself will have an experience of your own if you choose to visit Fort Reno. It would be a trip worth making.

The Cavalry Museum at Fort Reno

The present-day Cavalry Museum, which is open to visitors, is the oldest structure on the grounds of Fort Reno. It was originally built as a housing duplex for officers and their families. Residents lived in the structure from 1876 to 1948 before it sat vacant for many years. Finally, in 2014, as the structure was nearing demolition, the U.S. Cavalry Association raised the funds to restore the building and open it to the public by April 2015. The Cavalry Museum at Fort Reno is now the national headquarters for the U.S. Cavalry Association, and it houses items from saddles to service uniforms and many other service-related artifacts. The museum stands east of the parade grounds and south of the Visitor's Center and Museum. The restored two-story building features an enclosed porch that spans the entire front of the house. Upon entering, it becomes apparent that this building was restored with great care, from the original wood finishes to the artifacts displayed. As you enter the front of the building, you are greeted by a set of stairs that lead to the second floor. To the right is an open archway, which leads into a large open room filled with artifacts and memorabilia available for purchase. In this room, there is also a tour guide ready to assist visitors with any questions they may have. At the start of the tour, visitors are led upstairs and shown through various rooms. Each room holds its own theme or motif as it showcases items from the cavalry's past. From officers' living quarters to memorabilia from the Civil War, the museum truly takes its visitors back in time.

Before the duplex became a museum, several odd occurrences were reported. A worker at Fort Reno reported seeing lights on in the building even though there was no electricity. When restoration began on the building, workers on the outside of the second-story windows reported seeing a lady walk through the hallway in front of them and vanish through a wall.

Wendy Ogden, director and curator of the museum, told us a story from when she first started working at the museum. On the first day she was left alone, the fire alarms kept going off; this was not the usual chirp of a dying battery but a longer blip than that. After speaking to her boss, she was told that the fire alarms did not even have batteries but were hardwired into the house. After Wendy acknowledged the activity, it stopped. Two other museum workers reported the same activity on their first days alone in the house.

On many occasions, between the arrival of visitors and after hours, Wendy said she has felt the presence of a young child. She claimed that pencils have

Cavalry Museum. *Tanya McCoy.*

been knocked off desks, items have moved around frequently at about waist level and a flask flew off a shelf late one night when her kids were working in the office area. A volunteer said that he felt like he was going crazy when he heard children laughing throughout a tour he was giving a small family until the parents asked him, "Do you hear kids laughing?" Burial records show that a young boy named Louis Trass, an officer's son, died in April 1900 of unknown causes. Maria Wheeler, the daughter of a widow, passed in a house fire in the home that used to stand just north of the museum. Louis and Maria are now buried next to each other in the fort's cemetery.

On one occasion, a patron of the museum was so shaken by an experience during her visit that she drove to a diner to write it down and bring it back to the museum. Wendy said everything was normal that day. A couple had come in and was walking through the second floor at a normal pace when, all of sudden, they came running downstairs. The female visitor said she heard someone choking and swore it was Wendy behind her. However, when she turned to ask if Wendy was okay, she realized that no one was behind her.

As the director of the museum, Wendy has spent many nights working on the site. She said that, on one night in particular, she had a strange experience. Her thirteen-year-old son was with her as she was finishing up the workday, and the two left the museum at approximately eleven o'clock at night. As she drove down the road to leave the fort, her son began to frantically tell her that something was in the middle of the road. Wendy didn't see anything and kept driving as he called out, "Mom!" Her son then let out a sigh of relief and said, "Thank God. It stepped to the left." Wendy never saw anything in the road, but as soon as they returned home, her son drew a picture of what he had seen: a man, who appeared to have no arms, in military clothes. Later in the week, Wendy's son returned to the museum, and there were reenactors practicing on the parade grounds. As her son watched the reenactors, he recognized the "at ease" posture of the soldiers from what he had seen the night that the man stood in the road. Wendy said that they traveled back to where he saw the man and realized that the spot on the road where the apparition had stood was the marked location of the original gate to the fort. Perhaps a soldier's sense of duty never dies.

Wendy said that she also encounters many who claim to be psychics, mediums and sensitives. She said these visits can be interesting, but on several occasions, the same topic has been mentioned: "Someone here is unhappy about an item in the museum." After a number of these encounters, a lady approached Wendy about the item. She offered to show the woman the item that was likely the source of this entity's frustration, so the woman followed her to the saddle room. As the two women stood in front of a specific saddle, the straps began to sway on their own. This particular saddle was, in fact, not a cavalry saddle but one that an officer's daughter had used as part of a traveling circus. The traveling circus saddle is still in the museum.

Paranormal teams have visited the museum with equipment before and have gotten EVP recording. It is said that on some nights, after hours, chatter can be heard, but no one can make out the conversation. Ron Cross, founder of PROS Investigations, was in charge of one of the first paranormal teams to assist in developing the ghost tours held at the fort. Prior to the opening of the Cavalry Museum, Ron's team had a chance to investigate the building. He remembered one night, when he and two others were investigating, that they decided to conduct the "knock test," which is when an investigator knocks a certain number of times or in a well-known tune to see if the spirit will answer back. That night, the spirit was happy to comply. Ron said they asked the spirit to knock three times and gave an example. They all immediately heard the three knocks mere feet away from them. The team tried the experiment again, only to receive the same response. Is this definite proof that the building is haunted? No, but it does make one wonder who could have made those three loud knocks so many years ago.

Before visiting the museum, I did not know much about it other than the fact that it's a cavalry museum and that the spirits of two children were likely hanging around it. Upon arriving, I was invited to look around and get a feel for the building. While walking upstairs, I felt I did encounter a lady, who seemed like an overseer of things. While walking through the

Fort Reno military scouts. *Fort Reno.*

rooms, I heard footsteps in the room next to me, even though I was alone upstairs. I did not pick up on the spirit of a young boy until a little later. As I was sitting in the office speaking to Wendy, and as my three-year-old was pacing back and forth, oblivious to everything, the spirit peeked out from the hallway across from us, almost as if he was curious. Are the spirits of this house trying to get our attention? Are they trying to give a message, or are they just returning to a familiar spot? Perhaps a visit to the museum could help you answer those questions.

The Chapel of Fort Reno

Just northwest of the welcome center, there is an old, European-style chapel that was built in 1944 by a group of German prisoners of war (POWs). A shield of arms still graces the chapel today as a reminder of the craftsmen who labored to build the chapel so many years ago.

On July 4, 1943, during World War II, the first German POWs arrived at Fort Reno by rail. Most of the prisoners were from General Rommel's Afrika Korps and were captured in North Africa. These prisoners were given various jobs around the fort, and some were even hired out as farmhands to neighboring farms. The farmers would pay the government one dollar and fifty cents per day for the prisoners' labor, and in return, the government would pay the prisoners ten cents an hour in company scrip for them to purchase various goods at the canteen. The German prisoners were allowed far more luxuries at Fort Reno than American prisoners were in Germany. Prisoners at the fort were able to purchase two beers a day along with cigarettes and various other goods. When the prisoners left the fort to work on the farms, they were able pack a sack lunch to take with them, and many of the farmers also provided food or snacks for them. When they returned to Germany after the war, many of them remained in touch with the American farmers. Today, there are around seventy German POWs buried at the cemetery, but only one of those buried actually died at Fort Reno. The prisoners left a lasting mark on Fort Reno. From the trees lining the fort's driveway, to the beauty of the white chapel, Fort Reno displays the unity shared between the American soldiers, farmers and POWs during a difficult time in our country's history.

Today, as visitors arrive at the chapel, they are able to witness the contrast of the white chapel walls against a light blue sky. The dark wooden doors

Chapel at Fort Reno. *Tanya McCoy.*

with their cast-iron hinges and the square turret located on the east side of the building give the chapel a medieval feel. As visitors approach the set of heavy wooden doors, they take a step back in time as they step through the entryway. Wood floors are seen throughout the upstairs sanctuary, and solid, carved wooden benches line each side of the aisle. Cross timbers support the high-arched ceiling, and carved, wooden chandeliers adorn the hall. A wooden pulpit sits below the curved archway that outlines the stage, and a wooden hand-carved cross adorns the wall directly behind it. Arched glass windows line the walls and allow the sun to cast eerie shadows across the floor. At the front of the sanctuary, to the west of the pulpit, there is an open doorway that leads to an office located just behind the stage as well as to a narrow staircase that leads down into the basement of

Haunted El Reno

Prisoners of war at Fort Reno. *Fort Reno.*

the building. Short ceilings and round steel beams support the sanctuary above. In the basement, there is a small kitchen and an open area for tables for a wedding or an event.

Several years ago, I was fascinated with the history as well as the paranormal stories associated with the site, so I decided to hold one of our paranormal conferences at the old chapel. The conference was a weekend filled with great speakers, investigations, vendors and a psychic gallery reading. As usual, things did not always go as planned, but everything worked out, and before we knew it, the event was over. After all the guests had left and the vendors had packed up and gone, I found myself alone in the basement of the chapel doing some last-minute cleaning when I heard what sounded like someone walking around upstairs. Since I was responsible

Prisoners of war at Fort Reno. *Fort Reno.*

for the site, I quickly went upstairs to see who was still in the building, but no one was there. The front doors were still locked, and the only way to exit would have been to take the stairs down into the basement—the exact ones I had just come up. I had not noticed someone pass me on the stairs, and since they were so narrow, it would have been hard for someone to do it at all. I quickly walked around upstairs, looking down all the aisle seats, the changing room and the office. No one was in the building with me—well, at least not anyone living. I definitely did not feel alone. I descended the stairs into the basement and ascended the outside staircase to meet the rest of my group at the car. I told them about what I had just experienced. They had assured me that they were by my car, which was parked next to the basement door. No one had been seen entering or leaving the building but me.

I know what I heard that day; I heard the heavy footsteps of an unseen presence plainly as they echoed throughout the building. I have no explanation for where they came from, but I do know that something or someone was there with me that day. Could it have been one of the prisoners who helped to build the chapel so many years ago? Does the wood and mortar hold their energy from the past that they skillfully carved the edges into the wood? The old chapel holds a special feeling all its own, and it is just waiting for you to pass through the archway of its wooden doors.

The Victorian House at Fort Reno

On the northeast corner of the Fort Reno grounds sits an old Victorian house. The three-story home was built in 1889 for the daughter of a wealthy man who was unhappy with living in a tent at the fort. It is said that she would write home to her father complaining about how miserable her living conditions were. She was used to the finer things in life, and she quickly realized that being the wife of a military officer had its drawbacks. Soon after receiving her letters, her father shipped all the goods necessary to build his little girl a better home at the fort. Only the best building materials were used in the construction of the home, and it is one of the few original buildings left standing today. The home had fallen into some disrepair over the decades, but thanks to a special group of people that help preserve Fort Reno's history, this home has been restored to its former glory.

The house is large, with several rooms on the first level. Just inside the front door, there is a grand staircase that leads up to the second floor and an old brick fireplace that can be seen as you peer through the time-worn glass windows. This home is not open to tours, but guests can walk around the white-painted porch and peer into several windows to catch a glimpse of what the house looks like today. One can only imagine the dinner parties and afternoon teas that must have taken place there so many years ago.

The Victorian house is considered to be one of the most haunted buildings at Fort Reno even though it is not open to public investigations. Ron Cross, a former Fort Reno employee, shared with us some of the experiences had while leading ghost tours there many years ago. It was around 2006 or 2007 when Ron first contacted the historical society at the fort. He had heard that they were doing ghost tours, so he and his group volunteered to assist with them. While helping with the tours, his group was able to investigate

Victorian house at Fort Reno. *Tanya McCoy.*

inside the home, and he recalled an incident they had one night while investigating. He said that he and one of his team members, Jessica, were standing about twelve feet away from the stairs while some of his other team members were investigating another part of the home. Jessica was talking to Ron when he looked over toward the staircase and saw a full-body apparition of a woman standing in a long, white dress. Ron said he stared at the apparition in disbelief for several moments before the woman simply disappeared. As he was turned toward Jessica to see if she had seen the woman standing on the staircase, one of his other team members came down the stairs to ask them if they had been standing on the staircase. Ron said that it seemed they, too, had seen the mysterious lady in white.

Another spirit that appears around the house is that of a little girl. It is said that she doesn't show herself to just anyone; she only likes for other children to know of her presence. There have been several reports from parents over the years that said their children waved to something in one of the second floor's windows. When they asked their children what they are waving at, they would always reply, "The little girl who is waving at me." Children have also reported seeing a girl playing around the house in the yard, as well as on the porch.

Another presence has also been felt in the home, that of a male. Many people have reported feeling as if there is a man standing behind or near them, but no one has ever reported seeing him. The basement of the house also has strange occurrences. It is reported that a strong cigarette smell will appear out of nowhere. Ron's team had an experience in the basement. While doing an investigation, a strong smell of cigarette smoke filled the air. Ron went outside to look around the house to see if anyone was smoking, but no one was there.

Ron said he also experienced another paranormal event at the Victorian house, or rather, directly outside of the house. It was a windy night, which should come as no surprise to anyone who lives in Oklahoma, and a door on the building directly across from the house had not been closed properly. The door began to bang in the wind, causing a lot of noise contamination,

Haunted El Reno

Victorian house at Fort Reno. *Tanya McCoy.*

so one of the team members said she was going to the other building to close the door more securely. Ron said he volunteered do it instead, because he did not want her to go out by herself. It had been raining outside, so he grabbed his umbrella and headed toward the other building. There was a tall tree between the two buildings, and as he passed under it, he felt something pulling on his umbrella. He thought he had snagged it on one of the tree limbs, but as he turned around, he noticed the tree limbs were too high to even touch his umbrella. He continued to feel the tug on his umbrella, but due to the direction it was being pulled, he knew it couldn't have been the pull of the wind. As he turned to proceed toward the building, he looked down and noticed three skunks directly in his path. Had he not had to stopped due for the pulling on his umbrella, he would have walked directly into their paths. Was the spirit trying to warn him of the impending danger? Lucky for him, the spirit was in the right place at the right time.

Ron told us of another incident that happened to a group of visitors that came to the fort. He said that a group of teenage girls was standing in front of the house to take a group picture. Later, when they were looking through the photos, they noticed a woman standing on the porch in the background. They sent the picture to the Fort Reno Museum, and I was lucky enough to see it. It was as the group had said: Standing directly behind them was a full-body apparition of a woman in a long dress that reached the ground. Her hair was up in what appeared to be a bun, and she was standing with her hands on her hips, facing out to where the girls were standing. The girls claimed that no one else was there when the picture was taken, and in my personal opinion, the woman appeared to be wearing period clothing that could not be replicated today. Could this woman in the long dress possibly be the spirit that so many people have witnessed over the years, and if so, why does she choose to stay at the home? Did something horrific happen here, or did she love her home so much that she simply chose to stay? If you find yourself visiting Fort Reno, make sure you stop and take a look at the old Victorian house. Maybe you will be lucky enough to see the woman of the house. Just be careful and watch your step; you don't want to run into any skunks while you're there.

Fort Reno Cemetery

On a gravel road, just west of the fort, there is a waist-high stone wall that surrounds the Fort Reno Cemetery. The cemetery is the final resting place of military personnel, civilian employees and their families and prisoners of war from World War II. Of the nearly two hundred graves, approximately one-third are those of soldiers, most of whom did not die in battle.

The traditional opinion of cemeteries is that they are all creepy and eerie places. However, I find that most are quite peaceful places. I have visited the Fort Reno Cemetery before, sometime during high school, and remember it being my favorite part of the fort; I've always been a fan of old grave markers. The last time I visited the cemetery, I felt different as I walked up to its modest gate. The difference may have been that I actually knew some of the history of the fort and its function, and let's face it, people appreciate history more with age. It was a windy day, not surprising for the plains. I

Fort Reno Cemetery. *Tanya McCoy.*

almost did not want to sign the guest book for fear of pages the being ripped away, but I'm glad I did. I was able to see the signatures of visitors from all over, even from overseas, who had come here to pay their respects. Coins dotted the gravestones throughout the cemetery, placed there by men and women who had also served in the military. It was serene.

For years there have been reported sightings of a woman in white tucked between the cedar trees at the cemetery. I wondered who she might be. Is she buried there? Was she visiting a loved one who was buried here? Did she work at the fort? Could she have been Moka, the wife of the notable Indian scout Benjamin Clark, who is also interred at the fort's cemetery?

Benjamin Clark started his military career at the young age of thirteen as a post courier at Fort Bridger, Wyoming. He served in the Sixth Kansas

Cavalry during the Civil War, patrolling the Arkansas and Missouri borders. Following the Civil War, Clark managed pack trains and married his first wife, a Cheyenne woman known as Emily, who later gave birth to his first child, a girl named Jennie. Emily died in January 1873, and Clark remarried to a Cheyenne woman named Red Fern, with whom he had another child named Emily. Ben's second wife died in 1880, and he remarried later the same year to a woman named Moka, who was also known as "Little Woman." Clark and Moka had twelve children, five of whom died before 1900. Clark became fluent in the Cheyenne and Arapaho languages and was respected by Native Americans and white settlers alike. He joined the U.S. Army as a scout in 1868 and served as chief of scouts for General Philip Sheridan and Lieutenant Colonel George Custer. His third wife, Moka, died on May 6, 1913. After many years of service, the loss of his third wife and suffering from paralysis, Benjamin Clark ended his own life in his quarters at Fort Reno. That building, now called the Ben Clark House by staff, is still standing today, but it is not open to the public. Several people have reported a feeling of being choked when around the house.

The number of children buried here (fifty-six) is telling of the mortality rate for infants and children during the time that the fort was functioning. Perhaps the lady in white seen tucked between the trees still watches over them.

On the perimeter of the cemetery, a paranormal team that was leading a ghost tour recorded an EVP of someone saying, "I know, I know, I was run over." While searching through the fort's records, it was found that Tim O'Connell, an employee of the quartermaster department, was killed while helping three soldiers move to the fort on January 1, 1899. O'Connell was riding a mule when one of the soldiers hopped onto its back and startled the animal. Both of the riders were thrown, and O'Connell landed in front of a moving wagon, killing him almost instantly. He is buried in the fort's cemetery with a tombstone that simply reads "O'Connell."

Sightings of a full-body apparition of a male have been reported in the old commissary and armory building, which is not currently open to the public. Patrons and staff have reported seeing the same apparition, a young man asking them, "Is this a joke," at different times of the day. Some believe this apparition to be the spirit of a young soldier who died at the fort. On April 24, 1885, William Stockwell, who had not been feeling well, sought out the drug quinine. The only other personnel in the vicinity directed him to a bottle sitting on the windowsill. William questioned the substance inside but took a large dose after he was assured by several comrades that the contents

Haunted El Reno

Above: Ben Clark's home. *Tanya McCoy.*

Left: Fort Reno graves. *Tanya McCoy.*

Above: Old Commissary at Fort Reno. *Tanya McCoy.*

Left: POW graves. *Tanya McCoy.*

of the bottle were, indeed, quinine. Stockwell lived for two hours after taking this fatal dose. It was later confirmed by a doctor that the contents of that bottle were, in fact, strychnine. William was twenty-five years old when he died, and he was buried at the fort.

Perhaps the most somber part of the cemetery, aside from the many graves of children, is the western section. This section is the final resting place of 70 prisoners of war. During World War II, 1,300 POWs were brought to Fort Reno. Many of these POWs were from General Erwin Rommel's Afrika Korps that had been captured in North Africa. Many of the prisoners were hired as laborers at the fort and local farms. They built the chapel, which is still standing and open for tours today, in 1944. Of the 70 POWs buried here, only 1 actually died at the fort. Most of the others died in military camps around Oklahoma and Texas and were only brought to Fort Reno for burial.

LAKE EL RENO

There is a quaint little lake that sits just off I-40 to the west of El Reno. Named after the town itself, Lake El Reno was created in 1966 after the city recognized that there was a need for flood control and recreational facilities. The Four-Mile Creek flooded frequently, and when it did, it caused major damage to the town of El Reno. During the flood of 1953, approximately 475 homes and 25 businesses were affected when 353 acres of urban area became overrun by the floodwaters of the creek. Lake El Reno became part of the Watershed Project, a joint venture by the United States Soil Conservation Services and the City of El Reno to stop the flooding of Four-Mile Creek. The lake now covers a surface area of 170 acres and is surrounded by 4 miles of shoreline.

Today the lake offers camping, fishing and swimming, and the grounds contain an RV park, two large boat docks, a beach area, a walking trail, a picnic area, a disc golf course, a skate park, a playground, an ATV and off-road vehicle area and even a landing strip for remote-controlled planes. You can fish from the shoreline or the fishing dock as you stare out across the lake, watching as the sun sets just beyond the horizon. The lake offers a relaxing getaway from the daily hustle and bustle of life in the city.

When the sun sets and casts its last rays of golden light, the lake takes on a different feeling altogether. An eeriness creeps in, and darkness settles across the lake. On one such night, my team and I found ourselves visiting the lake for an investigation. Despite living only twenty miles away, I didn't know much about Lake El Reno. My team and I were scheduled for a private investigation of a historical home in El Reno when we found we had some extra time on our hands. Whitney suggested that we go out to the lake, because she had heard of several drownings in the area that may have produced some restless spirits.

We arrived just as the sun was starting to set. At first, we parked by the boat docking area and turned on our ghost radio to see if we could get anything to come through. We weren't getting much of a response in that location, so we decided to move on. We began to drive around the lake until we came upon the ATV area, where the road turned into a path of rocks and dirt. With thunderstorms cresting over the horizon, we decided not to venture off the road in case we got caught in a storm. I was trying to find a place to turn the car around when I noticed a white, see-through figure, approximately five feet tall, cross the road in front of us. It appeared to be a human form, but I was able to see directly through it as it crossed merely ten feet from our headlights. I tried to follow the figure as it walked into a wooded area, but I was no longer able to see it. The figure had walked toward the edge of the lake, but we didn't hear a splash or notice any movements in the water. This leads me to believe that the figure I had seen was only an animal, but it had been too tall to be a small rabbit or duck. There was no fog in the air that night, only rain clouds in the distance that were getting closer by the minute. Lightning started to light the sky and thunder rumbled off in the distance, so we started to drive back around the lake. We continued to ask questions in hope of getting a response from any spirit that might reside at the lake.

It wasn't long before my questions about the figure began to be answered through the ghost radio. My team and I decided to once again ask who we were speaking to, and the ghost radio responded, "Hunter." At that moment, Whitney and I looked at each other and both stated that we felt as if someone else had just taken a seat in the back of the car. Whitney then asked me if I had reached over and played with her hair, because she had felt someone lightly tugging on her hair. I assured her that I had not, but at that point, we both knew we were no longer alone in my car. We received several more responses from the ghost radio, one of which was, "being chased," but we were unable to decipher what those words meant at that time. With the storm and our scheduled investigation getting closer, we decided to end our makeshift investigation and made a mental note that a return visit to the lake would be warranted.

A few days later, I asked some of the residents of El Reno if they had ever experienced anything paranormal at the lake and was surprised at how many responses I received. I explained my experience to them, and it appears I am

ATV area at Lake El Reno. *Tanya McCoy.*

not the only one who has experienced some type of paranormal activity in that same area.

Feeling validated in my experience at the lake, I decided to do some research on the area. I was able to locate several accounts of drownings around the lake, as well as other accidents that include a few highway accidents near the area where I saw my ghostly apparition. Is it possible that the spirits of these victims still haunt the dark waters of the lake, or are these spirits from a time when the Wild West was being formed into the town we know today? If you are ever up for a relaxing day at the lake or for a ghostly investigation at night, I suggest you visit Lake El Reno. Just remember, if you go looking, you never know exactly who or what you might find!

The Southern Hotel

The Southern Hotel, located just off South Grand Avenue, was built in 1909 and was one of the state's largest and finest hotels during Oklahoma's early statehood. Standing three stories tall, this dark, brick building sports a white colonnade with a balcony on its face. The hotel was built to be fireproof and contains 125 rooms, 80 bathrooms, a grand staircase and an elevator.

In its early days, the hotel sat directly across the street from the Rock Island Railroad Depot, which would often receive an average of twenty-three passenger trains per day. Many of the railroad's passengers would stay at the hotel during layovers, which helped to bring business to the hotel. The depot had its own diner made up of two of its railway cars, but around the 1920s, the hotel and railway struck a deal that said the hotel would offer dining to all railway passengers. The hotel even provided a covered walkway between the depot and the hotel and established a terminal in the old wing of the hotel. The railway line was abandoned in 1946 due to the rise of the automobile industry, but the Southern Hotel remained busy. Some of the hotel's busiest times were during World War I and World War II, when soldiers were passing through El Reno on their way to various military bases around the United States. The hotel also played host to a number of social events such as political gatherings, dances and banquets.

Despite this success, in 1979, the once great building was starting to fall into disrepair when a developer stepped in to restore the building. No longer a hotel, the historic building housed offices, shops and even apartments. At

The Southern Hotel. *Tommy Neathery.*

one point, the building even stored a private collection of old, mint-condition cars in the basement. The building would later be transformed again into a senior citizens' center and retirement home, which is how it would stay for several decades.

The Southern Hotel was left to Myrtle Jackson by her family after their passing. She lived in Guthrie at the time and owned several properties, including a co-op publishing company. Myrtle had no real interest in the building, so she sold it to a woman named Goldie Jackson Ponds before running off with Goldie's husband and leaving her son to manage the hotel. Myrtle's son continued to manage the building until his death, which is steeped with mystery and suspense.

Goldie also never had much interest in the building, but she had purchased it for her nephew, Myrtle's son, who wished to continue to live there and run the place. Goldie was a devout spiritualist and often traveled to large spiritualist gatherings around the country. When she hired a woman named Judy, Goldie told her that she had been shown a picture of her and told that she needed to hire her to help her nephew run the hotel by a spirit. Goldie's nephew was not very responsible, and being somewhat of a party man, he hosted several parties. It is even said that during one of his drunken stupors, a guest of his tricked him into signing away ownership to all the classic cars stored in the hotel's basement. His mother ended up having to go to court

The Southern Hotel. *Tommy Neathery.*

to regain ownership of the cars. His party days continued, however, and he would often have guests over, some of whom were shady, to consume copious amounts of alcohol and drugs. Soon, Judy found herself taking on more and more of the responsibilities of the hotel. Goldie's nephew ended up going blind, and just before he died in the hospital, he woke up saying, "Don't shoot me in the neck anymore!" His final words left many people suspicious of his true cause of death.

During Judy's time at the hotel, she said she found several people in there who had passed away. Judy claimed that she was the one that found a past resident of the Southern Hotel, Robert Colby, or "Bob" as everyone called him, in his room. Bob was a retired farrier from Fort Reno who lived on the third floor of the Southern Hotel, where he was found dead in his room from natural causes. Another man, by the name of Blacky Blair, was also found dead in his room by Judy. She said she had returned to the Southern Hotel to find two of Blair's friends waiting for him in the lobby. They said that they were supposed to go out to eat that day, but he was late coming downstairs. Judy went up to check on him and found him dead, lying across his bed. It appeared as if he had just stood up and fell back onto the bed, dead at that moment. Other bodies have also been discovered at the Southern Hotel, many of them being transients who just happened to pass away on the property. I asked Judy if she ever experienced any paranormal activity while she worked there, but she replied that she was always too busy trying to take care of the building to notice anything else. Judy may not have experienced any paranormal activity herself, but many other people have come forward with their experiences over the years.

Every historic building comes with a handful of ghost stories, and the Southern Hotel is no different. Several people have reported encounters with some of the hotel's spirits. From phantom bellhops to music playing from unseen origins, the Southern Hotel seems to have it all. These are some of the tales from former tenants and residents who met a few guests of the hotel who never wished to leave.

One previous resident told me of an experience she had while living in an apartment there. She said was lying in bed one night when she heard what appeared to be a man's voice coming from one of the other rooms. Since she lived alone at the time, she became very scared thinking that someone had broken into her apartment. This incident also took place in a time before cellphones, so calling the police wasn't an option unless she made it to the phone in the other room. She quietly crept out of bed and tried to look through the crack of her bedroom door to see where the voice come from, but there was no one there. She gently opened the door and took another look around. She turned on the lights and saw that nothing looked out of place and her front door was still locked from the inside. She decided she must have been dreaming and returned to bed. She didn't think much more about the incident until the next night. She had just put down her book and was reaching over to turn out the light when she heard a man's voice whisper, "I'm here," into her ear. She jumped out of bed and ran from the room. She knocked on her neighbor's door and told her what she had experienced. They both returned to the apartment to check things out, but once again, there was no one to be seen. She didn't sleep at all that night, and she had kept all of her lights on.

When she went to work the next day, her co-workers could tell that she was upset and asked her what was wrong. She told them about her experiences from the previous two nights in her apartment and about how scared she was to return. One of her co-workers agreed to go home with her to check the place out. Nothing happened while they were at the apartment that evening, but later that night, the activity began again. She had just gone to bed and had again decided to sleep with the light on that night. Just as she started to close her eyes, she could feel a movement on the bed as if someone had sat down. She immediately got out of the bed, grabbed her clothes and left, heading over to a friend's house for the night. A few days later, she returned to her apartment with a friend and performed a blessing on the apartment. She said things quieted down after that, but it took her awhile before she was comfortable being alone in the apartment again.

Nancy Everett-Salsman also told me her story from when her father, Fred Everett, owned a secondhand store known then as Fred's Second-Hand Shop in the old hotel's building in the 1970s. Nancy describes the building's floor as being covered in an old, black-and-white checkered pattern. She remembers him telling her that when he wasn't busy, he would often pass time sitting and talking with the ghosts in the building. I wonder if they ever talked back?

Other paranormal encounters reported at the hotel involve the ghostly apparition of a bellhop. One past resident told me her story of when she came face-to-face with this spirit of the hotel's past. She said she had just arrived home from work and was climbing the stairs to the second floor when she glanced over and noticed a man standing next to her. She said that the man was staring at her with very intent eyes, and the hairs on the back of her neck started to stand on end as a feeling of uneasiness started to come over her. She had never seen the man before, and there was something about him that didn't feel right. He didn't speak a word to her, just continued to stare. She nodded to him and said hello, but he never answered back. As she turned to walk toward her apartment, she quickly looked back over her shoulder, but he was gone. She looked over the railing to see if he had gone downstairs, but there was nothing there. He had simply vanished.

A few days later, she was telling a friend about her experience when her friend asked her to describe the man she had seen. After describing the man, her friend told her the man she had described sounded just like the old bellhop that used to work at the hotel. Her friend also informed her that he had died several years before. Even though she never felt threatened by the entity that she had seen that night, the former resident was happy that she never ran into him again.

Now, the historic building is getting another upgrade. The building will once again offer senior living, but it will also now offer low-rent apartments for teens who are aging out of the foster care system and are homeless or at risk of becoming homeless. The development will include case management services, a fitness room, a computer room and a group kitchen in the hopes of providing a sense of community between El Reno's elderly and youth. Once again, this historic building will be one of the finest places in El Reno, not just because of the building itself, but for the wonderful services it will provide.

The Whistle Stop Saloon

Sitting on the corner of Wade and Grand Streets is a small two-story building known as the Whistle Stop Saloon. It's a quaint bar where many locals have gone to hang their hats after long days for the past several decades. Through the front door, there is an old, wooden bar top, surrounded by tall chairs waiting for the next guest to come for a cold drink. In the back of the bar there is a large mirror surrounded by dark, hand-carved wood with a design to give the feel of the old western days. On the side of the building there is a set of old wooden stairs that leads to the second floor. This level of the building contains an apartment that has been occupied by several residents in the past. To date, there have been at least three recorded deaths in the apartments. It is not uncommon for people to pass away in apartments, homes and hotels, but when paranormal activity occurs afterward, it can be somewhat unnerving.

The saloon isn't large, but what it lacks in space, it makes up for in character. You won't find any loud music or a bunch of thugs wanting to throw their weight around there. No, you will only find a bunch of guys relaxing after a day of work at the Whistle Stop Saloon. It's the kind of place you would expect someone to know you by your name. Built in the early 1900s, the Whistle Stop Saloon hasn't always been a pub. In 1909, the building was a small café called the Eagle Café, and it was owned by a man named Connors. As the years passed, the building also became a general store before it was finally turned into a bar known as the Office Tavern. It would remain under that name for several years until it was bought by

Haunted El Reno

The Whistle Stop Saloon. *Tanya McCoy.*

Barbara, who would rename it to Gallagher's Pub. Years later, when Barbara sold the business to her daughter, Nikki, she changed the name to the current Whistle Stop Saloon.

The Whistle Stop Saloon's paranormal activity was first witnessed when it was still Gallagher's Pub. Barbara, the previous owner, shared some of her stories with me. She said that many people reported the smell of an old woman's perfume that wouldn't be worn today, and Barbara said she could often smell the same perfume in the apartment upstairs. She said there were also reports of a dark, shadowy figure standing in the closet of the bathroom in the bar. On the bar's cameras, Barbara said she would notice a lot of orb activity, and she said they could often see orbs with their own eyes, off the camera. Patrons reported pool balls moving on their own and the jukebox playing music without anyone turning it on. Barbara stated that her own niece was afraid to walk down the hallway alone in the apartment upstairs.

A few years back, I was invited out to the bar, when it was still known as Gallagher's Pub, to do a book signing and to talk about my paranormal investigations for a Halloween event. Even then, I could tell that this location had a special feel to it. I could feel the female presence haunting the building in the bar that night. She did not cause any mischief; she was simply visiting to join in the festivities. Despite being haunted, the Whistle Stop Saloon doesn't possess an eerie feeling. It is a place for locals to just sit, relax and have a good time. If you visit the saloon and start to smell an old lady's perfume, pull up a chair and offer her a drink. After all, we all need a few spirits now and then.

DOWNTOWN EL RENO AND MAIN STREET HAUNTINGS

HAUNTED ROCK ISLAND AVENUE

Located in historic downtown El Reno, Rock Island Avenue is one of the main streets that leads into the very heart of the town. This street was once the soul and center of El Reno, but due to growth and expansion, many businesses have migrated away from the area, leaving many of its historic buildings vacant. The beauty of these buildings remains despite the emptiness of them. The aging of the old brick and mortar doesn't take away from the buildings' elegance and beauty, in fact, it enhances it. Their age makes the buildings unique, and it helps them stand out among the plainness of most modern-day shops. A historic building is a wonderful location a business, but with some of these buildings, you might get a little more than you bargained for.

    Many historic buildings are known to harbor a few ghosts, and many of the buildings along Rock Island Avenue seem to host a few of their own. One such building is the old Rock Island Office itself. Standing in the middle of the South 100 block of Rock Island Avenue is a two-story, red brick building. The office was built between 1889 and 1890 and displays the common red brick outer walls and large front windows of structures built during that period. On the first floor of the building is an area that has often been used as storefront. For many years, it held a women's clothing store. The owner's mother shared her stories with us from when she worked there in the 1970s. She said the building was a wonderful place to work, and her

A.F. Newell Department Store at 110 North Rock Island Avenue. *Tommy Neathery.*

friends from around town would often come to visit her. She told us they would often sit around the cash register and gossip about things going on around town, smoking and laughing and having a great time. Over the next couple of decades, the building hosted a number of other stores, including a secondhand store and a game store. Currently, the location sits empty, but, hopefully, that will not be the case for long.

I went to look at this location as a potential site for my team's future haunted museum, and I fell in love with it immediately. The storefront has a welcoming atmosphere, it's large and welcoming, measuring 2,300 square feet in size, and even though it currently sits empty, there is more to it than meets the eye. The cracking black-and-white tile and aging wallpaper are not the only things that remain from this building's past. There is an energy that can be felt lingering around the building. It isn't a menacing feeling and it doesn't feel frightening in the least, but some there is some type of energy that remains there.

After looking around the downstairs area, the current owner agreed to take me to the second floor of the building, which was used as the original

Old Rock Island administration offices. *Tanya McCoy.*

Rock Island Railroad administration office. In order to reach the second level, we had to exit the storefront and walk past the building next door. Once, this area was simply a breezeway, or an alley of sorts, but it has since been converted to an enclosed staircase. The stairs leading up to the second level are very old and appear unsteady. Old, rusty nails can be seen trying to work their way out of the aging boards, and the dust and cobwebs lining the stairs only add to the eerie feeling of the stairs. In the old office space, the original floors and woodwork are still intact. Open doorways are scattered throughout the large, open area, and the tall windows at the front of the building help to illuminate some of the office, but most of it remains hidden in shadow.

The ceiling of the office is high and vaulted, and the old, thin slats of wood can be seen lining some of the building's walls. Bits and pieces of the building's mortar have begun to crumble from the aging walls and are scattered around on the floor. One large room still holds black soot on the walls from when it had once caught fire. As the owner and I walked through the building, I knew there was someone or something else there. I turned on my ghost radar application to see what we could find as we continued on our tour. As soon as we walked out of the burned room, the radio said, "Let me out." The owner said they weren't sure if anyone had ever died in the building or had even passed away during the fire, but one thing is for certain, we were not alone. I am hoping to return to this location in the future to find out who is still haunting the old Rock Island Railroad office and why.

The Bakery

Located just a few doors down from the old Rock Island Administration office, there is another small shop with a history of a hauntings. As you enter the shop, you can see that it is shaped like a long rectangle, like so many other buildings of its period. The floor has old-fashioned black and white tiles set in a checkered pattern, and the walls are lined with inlaid glass shelving to display various goods. Toward the back of the shop is a counter top where the register or check-out area would be. This location has recently been rented out to a bakery that offers delicious treats, such as fruit tarts and specialty cakes. Prior to it housing a bakery, the building was home to Butt's Flowers, and it was during that time that the paranormal activity was first reported. Amber, the owner of Butt's Flowers, said that they would often witness the sound of little girls giggling throughout the building. She even reported hearing what sounded like children running through the building, even when there were no children around. The disembodied giggles were heard several times, but the spirits never appeared to them.

The Main Street Office

Just down from the bakery is the present Main Street Office. Like many buildings downtown, this location has been home to its fair share of various businesses. This location was once home to a travel company, a plumbing company and even the site of the city's first jail. Now, the city is using it as the Main Street Office in hopes of bringing more business to the historic downtown area. The front of the office is relatively small in size, hosting only one desk and a table for meetings. I met the current and the previous managers of the Main Street Office in the hope of gathering some more information about the buildings in downtown El Reno. They were very helpful, and Debbie, a past employee, reminded me of an incident that we had experienced a few years before, when I had last come to visit her. We were preparing to host a paranormal event in El Reno, and we were looking into areas to host the event around the town. We were told that the current Main Street Office building had some paranormal stories attached to it, and we were invited to take a look. We were shown to the back of the building, which was a large, open area that was being used for storage at the time. The area definitely had a feeling to it, and it didn't take long for the psychic that was with us that day to start picking up on an entity. She said she could see a woman in a wedding dress who was sad because she was being forced to marry a man she didn't love. The entity said that he was much older than her, but he was very wealthy. The psychic believed she might have killed herself,

The Main Street Office. *Tanya McCoy.*

which was why she was still haunting the building. Now, keep in mind, to this day, we have not been able to credit or discredit what the psychic said she witnessed, but I can tell you that this building does have strange feeling to it when you walk in that area. Hopefully, in the future, we will be able to further investigate the Main Street Office.

Bickford Avenue

The other main street in downtown El Reno is Bickford Avenue. Bickford is a one-way street that houses another large group of historic buildings. One of these buildings is the Centre Theater, which was given a story all on its own. However, there are several more haunted buildings lining this old street.

One such building is located directly next to the Centre Theater, and it is known as Our Glass, a quaint little pub that has been renovated to host small gatherings and even live music from time to time. It has a beautifully remodeled interior with a brick inlay for various wines and a beautiful old-fashioned wood bar. Tables are placed around for guests to enjoy a meal or snack, and at the front of the pub, there is a small stage surrounded by cozy chairs and couches for the guests to sit back and enjoy music. During our investigation of the Centre Theater, we received several messages about the pub next door and decided to check it out. I spoke to the owner, who said they hadn't been in the building long, but he said his daughter often claimed she would get a weird feeling when they were in the building. We have been invited to come and investigate the pub, but unfortunately, we were not able to investigate in time for this book. I will say that agree with the daughter. I believe that there is possibly something or someone still hanging around this old pub, and I look forward to finding out exactly what or who it might be.

Another haunted building on Bickford Avenue is the old Russell Murry Hospice building. This building is one of El Reno's many saloons from the old days that was rumored to have housed a brothel on the second floor. Many of the building's past employees reported feeling an uneasiness in the building, and many of them did not like the area upstairs.

The Blu 99 is also rumored to have spirits lingering around the old building, especially on the upper floors. This old, three-story, red brick building has been around since the late 1800s and has housed many different businesses throughout the years. Old photographs can be seen of children sitting on the

Photo of downtown El Reno during a parade in 1936. *Tommy Neathery.*

Photo of Bickford Avenue with the Masonic lodge. *Tommy Neathery.*

windowsills, watching as parades passed on the streets below. Today, it serves as a quaint boutique for visitors to enjoy.

The old Masonic Temple is also located on Bickford Avenue, one block down from the Blu 99. It is a tall, three-story building that once housed a department store on its lower level. The upper level housed the

The Grand Opera located off Bickford Avenue. *Tommy Neathery.*

Masonic Temple, and the gate leading to the building's alleyway is marked with their symbol. That mark is the only piece of evidence marking this historic location. The alleyway itself has an intriguing feeling all its own. Sadly, I have been told that the second floor of this building is in disrepair and is very dangerous at this time, so it is best to steer clear of any possible investigations.

There are other buildings along Rock Island Avenue and Bickford Avenue that have haunted histories associated with it, but since they are current businesses, some owners are reluctant to share their stories for fear of people contacting them or trespassing. So, please be advised that the buildings listed here, and the others that line the street, are considered private property, and you will be prosecuted for trespassing or breaking and entering if you enter them without permission. This area is closely monitored, and the Canadian County Sheriff and the El Reno Police Departments are only a few blocks away.

The Heritage Apartments

Located on Watts Street, just south of the Canadian County Museum, is an old building known as the Heritage Apartments. Built in 1918, this three-story brick building was the first in El Reno to have an elevator and was home to the southern division offices of the Rock Island Railroad before the corporation went bankrupt around 1980. The building sat vacant for many years before it was transformed into an apartment complex. Once each office had its own door, the building was perfect for apartments. One current resident, Melissa Donnell, shared her stories with me from the time she lived on the second floor of the building. She said that she and her family would often see a red fog appear out of nowhere. She also said that she would often get an uneasy feeling, as if something was about to jump out at her, and that her family always felt like they were being watched.

Melissa wasn't the only resident to share a story with me. Another resident told me about some strange things that happened to him when he lived in the Heritage Apartments. He said that he was up late watching TV one night when something caught his eye. He noticed a strange movement by the doorway and turned just in time to see the silhouette of a man pass through the doorway to his bedroom. He jumped up, thinking that someone had broken into his apartment. He headed toward his room to confront the intruder, but when he got there, he saw no one. He also claimed that things would often come up missing, only to be found days later in places that he never would have left them.

Rock Island's old southern division office, which is currently known as the Heritage apartments. *Tanya McCoy.*

Mystery surrounds this old Rock Island Railroad building. We may never know the answer to some of the building's mysteries, but it holds over one hundred years of history that we will hopefully be able to enjoy for another hundred years. Perhaps we will even leave some of our own history behind.

The Old Canadian County Jail

Located on the corner of the three hundred block of South Evans Avenue is the old Canadian County Jail. Built between 1904 and 1907 by A.C. Kreipke, and designed by the noted Oklahoma architect Solomon Andrew Layton and his partner, W. J. Riley, this two-story building has withstood the test of time. The jail and its stables are the oldest public buildings in Canadian County that are still standing. The jail was built in the Italian Renaissance style and measures forty-seven feet by fifty-eight feet. Its T-shaped layout could house up to twenty-four male inmates at any given time. It also contained a female ward, a detention ward for boys and multiple offices. The structure is made of brick and consists of both smooth and rough surfaces, and large, bar-covered windows flank its outer walls. Two tall columns surround the rust-colored doors, and skinny, tall windows adorn its front. Window unit air-conditioners were added in the 1970s, and the old chimney stack can still be seen on top of the old roof.

The stables sit directly west of the old jail and were built between 1908 and 1913. The building is made of red bricks, and it stands two stories high. Bar-covered windows also line the outer walls of this building, along with a large, sliding door that is wide enough to get a horse and carriage through. Both buildings are listed in the National Register of Historic Places (NRHP).

The jail remained in use until the mid-1980s, when the second-floor jail cells had to be closed off due to the lack of a fire escape. The first level, however, remained open and was used as administration offices until 1986,

Old Canadian County Jail. *Tanya McCoy.*

Old Canadian County Jail, 1908. *Carnegie Library.*

when the new county jail was built. Since then, the building has been used as a storage area for records, seized drugs and guns. At the end of 2018, the building was cleared of all items in storage and was turned over to the preservation society.

The jail is a beautiful, historic building, but like most of the other older buildings in El Reno, it has a ghostly past. The late 1800s and early 1900s in the Oklahoma Territory were hard years for many people. Between the land run, early settlement and the displacement of the native tribes, life on the open frontier proved to be quite challenging and deadly. With the population growing daily, outlaws soon filled the Oklahoma Territory. From bank robbers and thieves to murderers, the county jail soon became home to many prisoners. El Reno played host to a wide variety of outlaws, including the Wild Bunch, also known as the Doolin-Dalton Gang, who held up an El Reno bank before making off with $17,000. With so much history of criminal activity, it comes as no surprise the old jail still holds on to some of the spirits from its past.

Some the paranormal activities associated with the old jailhouse are the sound of walking, disembodied voices and the movement of objects. Those who have been in the jail claim that they got an uneasy feeling when they entered the building. At this point, the building isn't open to the public, but perhaps, in time, we will all get a chance to meet some more of the ghosts from El Reno's past.

EL RENO CEMETERY

Located on the southeast side of El Reno is the El Reno Cemetery. On October 27, 1889, the first resident was laid to rest in the cemetery just five short months after the land run. A young man, at the tender age of seventeen, passed away from a condition known as typhoid. The first vault was erected in the cemetery in 1899, and several more impressive vaults have been added since that date. Despite the number of El Reno residents that were buried in the cemetery, the city did not own the property until April 9, 1900. The city payed one dollar and twenty-five cents per acre to acquire the eighty acres of the cemetery. As of a 2006 report, the cemetery has over sixteen thousand residents buried in it, and there is a strong possibility that there are several more unknown graves on its grounds.

The cemetery's layout is unique and designed in a true western style. The center of the cemetery has a long drive that splits off in several different directions, forming the shape of a wagon wheel. The cemetery has a very peaceful atmosphere that is quiet and serene. It's a beautiful place for a final rest. Like most cemeteries, it's peaceful during the day, but at night, it takes on somewhat different feeling.

Over the years, I have heard different stories surrounding the cemetery, but the one I remember the most is an encounter of my own. A few years ago, I worked with a pediatric patient on the night shift, and every night, on my way to work, I would drive by the El Reno Cemetery. Each night, I was drawn to it, as if I was being called, and I always looked at it as I passed by. One night, something caught my eye by the roundabout, standing just under the bright light of a street lamp. There, standing directly under the

Mausoleum at El Reno Cemetery. *Tanya McCoy.*

light, was a young lady. She was wearing a pale-colored dress that went about midway to her calves, and she had dark brown hair that ended just below her shoulders. She simply stared back at me, with no expression, and watched as I drove by. There was a sadness about her; she was so young and so pretty. I took a quick glance back at the street, and then back to where she was, but she was gone. I quickly scanned the rest of the cemetery, but she was nowhere in sight. I knew at that moment that I had seen a ghost. I never saw her again after that night, but every time I passed the cemetery, I could still feel someone watching me. I never found out who this mysterious woman was, and I know there is no hope of ever knowing who she is, but her face still haunts my memory. Perhaps, one day, she will show herself again and share her story with me. Until then, may she rest in peace.

BIBLIOGRAPHY

Barker, Carolyn. "Burials in the Fort Reno Cemetery, 1874–1948." www.files.usgwarchives.net
Benevolent and Protective Order of Elks. "Elks History Project: How the Elks Began." www.elks.org.
Canadian County Museum Historical Archives
Fort Reno. "Fort Reno Historical Information." www.fortreno.org.
Hoig, Stan. "*The Encyclopedia of Oklahoma History and Culture*—Fort Reno." www.okhistory.org.
National Park Service. "Ben Clark." www.nps.gov.
Savage, Cynthia. "*The Encyclopedia of Oklahoma History and Culture*—El Reno." www.okhistory.org.
The Shadow Lands. "Haunted Places in Oklahoma—Dead Man's Curb." www.theshadowlands.net.
———. "Haunted Places in Oklahoma—Route 66 to Weatherford." www.theshadowlands.net.

About the Authors

Tanya has been interested in the paranormal since she saw her first full-body apparition in her own home at the young age of six. She started doing research on the paranormal around 2001 and joined a paranormal investigation team around 2008. She started her own paranormal investigation team, the Oklahoma Paranormal Association (OPA), in 2011. As the founder of OPA and president of Paranormal Times Entertainments LLC, she is always teaching others and providing private investigations for public and private institutions. She has been featured on *My Ghost Story*, *Paranormal 911* and *Haunted Hospitals*, which are shows on the Syfy Channel and the Travel Channel, as well as many articles, podcasts and newscasts. She has coauthored three books: *Haunted Guthrie*, *Haunted Canadian County* and *Haunted Oklahoma City*. Along with speaking at a number of paranormal events in Oklahoma, she has started teaching her first paranormal class, Paranormal Psychology, at Francis Tuttle Metro Technology Centers. She hopes to develop a special textbook for future classes. She has a bachelor's degree in parapsychology and is currently working toward her PhD. Aside from investigating the paranormal, Tanya has been a pediatric nurse for the past twenty-one years and works with special needs children. She is also a published children's book author, wife and mother of three. She is currently working her next book, which will focus on her two favorite topics: history and the paranormal. She is also currently writing a mystery novel, three other children's books and two stage plays.

Whitney Wilson has a long history of paranormal experiences but had never been a member of a paranormal investigation team until she joined the Oklahoma Paranormal Association in 2015. She started out as a team member before advancing to her current position as the vice president of Paranormal Times Entertainments LLC and the Oklahoma Paranormal Association. Since joining the team, Whitney's quest for knowledge and understanding of the paranormal has grown substantially. She is the coauthor of *Haunted Canadian County*, and she says that it's great to be able to back up her experiences with actual history. Whitney is also a pediatric nurse, wife and mother.

www.ingramcontent.com/pod-product-compliance
Lightning Source LLC
Chambersburg PA
CBHW042144160426
43201CB00022B/2404